Baby Boomer Rock 'n' Roll Fans

The Music Never Ends

Joseph A. Kotarba

THE SCARECROW PRESS, INC.
Lanham • Toronto • Plymouth, UK
2013

Published by Scarecrow Press, Inc.
A wholly owned subsidiary of The Rowman & Littlefield Publishing Group, Inc.
4501 Forbes Boulevard, Suite 200, Lanham, Maryland 20706
www.rowman.com

10 Thornbury Road, Plymouth PL6 7PP, United Kingdom

Portions of this book originally appeared, in slightly different form, in the following publications: *Cultural Studies* (parts of chapter 3), *Qualitative Inquiry* (parts of chapter 7), and *Symbolic Interaction* (parts of chapter 8). Some of this material also appeared in edited collections by the author as well as his book *Understanding Society through Popular Music* (Routledge, 2009).

British Library Cataloguing in Publication Information Available

Library of Congress Cataloging-in-Publication Data

Joseph A. Kotarba
Baby boomer rock 'n' roll fans : the music never ends / Joseph A. Kotarba.
p. cm.
Includes bibliographical references and index.
ISBN 978-0-8108-8483-0 (cloth : alk. paper) — ISBN 978-0-8108-8484-7 (ebook) 1. Popular music—Social aspects. 2. Popular music fans. 3. Baby boom generation. I. Title.
ML3918.P67K65 2013
306.4'84260973—dc23
2012025712

♾™ The paper used in this publication meets the minimum requirements of American National Standard for Information Sciences Permanence of Paper for Printed Library Materials, ANSI/NISO Z39.48-1992.

Printed in the United States of America

Contents

Acknowledgments

Writing this book has been possible as a result of many people who have had patience with me and an appreciation for the value and magic of rock 'n' roll. The greatest supporters were those people who shared their music and their love of music with me: John Peterson, Nick Grygiel, Stan Beyderman, Cindi and Lou Ramon, Nolan Chambers, Matt Tomaszewski, Wayne Zawislak, Don Nolek, Mike Katovich, Phillip Vannini, Bryce Merrill, Chris Schneider, Joey Polys, and Rob Gardner, among many others.

Much of my work has been supported by artistic and scientific grants from the Texas Commission on the Arts, the Cultural Arts Council of Houston and Harris County, the Houston Arts Alliance, the University of Houston, the Joseph S. Werlin Fellowship in Latin American and Hispanic Studies, the National Endowment for the Arts, Texas State University–San Marcos, the Center for Social Inquiry at Texas State University, the National Institute on Drug Abuse, and the Texas Commission on Alcohol and Drug Abuse.

I want to thank Louis Messina from the Messina Group, Jeff Messina from the Warehouse Live in Houston, the staff at the Cynthia Woods Mitchell Pavilion in The Woodlands, and the staff at the Houston Livestock Show and Rodeo for providing me gracious access to a wide range of concerts, artists, staff members, and fans over the years.

I also want to thank my editor, Bennett Graff, for liking my manuscript enough to nurture it through publication.

I want to thank my good colleagues and friends in the Department of Sociology at Texas State University–San Marcos. They gave me a breath of fresh air, in more than one way, that helped me finish this project with energy and verve.

I dedicate this book to Chris, Jessie, and Andrew, who created a soundtrack for my life and my work through their saxophone, flute, and clarinet—the angels must play woodwinds—and . . .

To Polly, my firework.

ONE

Understanding Baby Boomers

The evening of September 24, 2010, was warm and breezy in Houston, Texas. The crowd at the Cynthia Woods Mitchell Pavilion was gathering just before sunset for the Tom Petty concert. The Mitchell Pavilion is a gorgeous setting for outdoor concerts. The stage is flanked by tall and stately southern pine trees and covered by a flowing white canopy—with multiple peaks—to provide welcomed shade to the performers and re-served-seat patrons alike. The unreserved seating is out on the lawn, which fans out on a rising hill. A few Frisbees could be seen crisscrossing the clear blue sky above the audience.

The audience was not, however, a typical rock 'n' roll audience—whatever that might be in our postmodern world. In fact, the 15,300 fans gathered there contributed to the increasing difficulty in deciphering just what a typical rock 'n' roll audience is. The audience was approximately 50 percent male and 50 percent female but overwhelmingly adult—no, specifically, middle-age or older. Most fans were in male-female couples, but there was a smattering of generational mix: a father with his teenaged son here, a teenaged daughter with her middle-age parents there. I even witnessed a dad playing Frisbee with his son while the band was setting up. The lawn was flooded with chairs rented for $20 a piece. There were relatively few fans sitting on blankets, given the lawn's incompatibility with often sore, increasingly fragile, and unquestionably aging backs. There appeared to be more fans drinking white wine than beer, and there were many sets of binoculars available to provide assistance for eyes weakened by age. Similarly, there were many ear plugs visible in the crowd to protect ears weakened, if not damaged, by too many years of loud rock 'n' roll. Of course, the lawn chairs, binoculars, earplugs, and white wine were all available at numerous concession stands.

1

The commons area just inside the entrance way was most notably marked by three significant symbols that served to define the situation. The first was the traditional T-shirt stand, which was also well stocked with Tom Petty CDs. The second was the kiosk covered with ads for satellite radio service. These ads were clearly directed to the mature and affluent music fan who has outgrown broadcast radio, with its overabundance of urban contemporary noise, very old oldies, and depressing talk shows. The third was a BMW sedan, all silver with silver leather upholstery and a silver iPod case with BMW logo. Put simply, the BMW was not anything like the VW "Flower Power" love bus that some of the audience members drove before they converted to and achieved the American Dream.

Anyone could gaze across the lawn and see middle-class rock 'n' roll fans, albeit aging rock 'n' roll fans. A sociologist can gaze across the lawn and see approximately 3,400 men who take Viagra or Cialis to restore their sexuality, almost 4,500 women and men who take high blood pressure to keep their cardiac systems young and functional, 2,100 men and women who take an aspirin a day to minimize the risk of stroke, almost 2,000 women and men who take statins to reduce their bad cholesterol levels, 900 men and women who have had cosmetic surgery or Botox treatments in an attempt to regain the appearance of youth, and at least 1,950 women who take calcium supplements to reduce the rate of bone loss. Approximately 3,000 fans have been married and divorced—and probably remarried.[1]

The baby boomers—born between 1945 and 1964—present at events such as this Tom Petty concert are getting old. Many professional and lay observers have noted in recent years the way that the baby boomer generation uses relationships, occupations, investments, religion, hobbies—and medicine—to accomplish one task: to forestall, master, and/or enhance the aging process (Kotarba 2011). The purpose in writing this book is to describe, sociologically, the many ways that people in our society who were raised on rock 'n' roll music and its cultural baggage have continued to use the rock 'n' roll idiom to make sense of, celebrate, and master everyday life—through adulthood and for the rest of their lives.

The scholarly literature on popular music in general, and rock 'n' roll in particular, has traditionally focused on music experiences among young audiences. Specifically, the focus has been on the rock 'n' roll idiom as a feature of adolescent culture and, therefore, teenagers' everyday life experience. As Simon Frith (1981) noted in his famous sociological text *Sound Effects*, rock 'n' roll music has been fundamental to the experience of growing up ever since the end of World War II. Similarly, sociologists have demonstrated increasing interest over the years in rock 'n' roll music as an indicator of dramatic changes occurring in the social and cultural worlds of teenagers. We can trace this interest at least as far back as David Riesman's (1950) classic examination of the emergence of the other-directed personality in post–World War II American society. The new middle class was marked by a weakening of parental control, a preoccupation with consumption, and a shift in the meaning of leisure, resulting in the masses—the lonely crowd—desperately trying to have fun. The time was ripe for the emergence of a youth culture defined by what has come to be known as rock 'n' roll music.

The popular music industry that markets rock 'n' roll continues to expand dramatically, if not always economically—beyond multibillion-dollar annual sales, globalization, CDs, MP3 technology, and the Internet. Yet, lay and scholarly observers have generally ignored or underplayed an important element of social and cultural change: rock 'n' roll is no longer limited to, nor solely the possession of, teenagers. The original generation of rock 'n' rollers—the baby boomers—are now parents and, increasingly, grandparents. The music and musical culture they grew up with has stayed with them, becoming the soundtrack of American culture.

I define rock 'n' roll music very broadly as a style of popular music that (1) is created for and marketed toward young people or people who consume music according to youthful tastes and values; (2) is primarily guitar driven and amplified; (3) has its musicological and cultural origins in African American musical styles; (4) is usually danceable; and (5) sounds best when played or performed loudly (Kotarba 1994a). I define rock 'n' roll broadly to include all varieties of pop music that have evolved from or are heavily influenced by it (e.g., heavy metal, pop, New Age, Christian pop, and even rap/hip-hop). All told, rock 'n' roll music—along with its musical, economic, and historical derivatives—arguably compose the preeminent form of popular music in our society.

Although many observers still assume that rock 'n' roll is essentially a feature of youth culture, I argue that it is a key feature of adult culture and a primary source of everyday meanings for the first generation raised on it. The concept of the existential self, which focuses on the situational and evolving aspects of individuality in a rapidly changing social world, informed several of my qualitative studies to produce the following ways to characterize personal rock 'n' roll experiences: the e-self, the self as lover, the self as parent, the self as believer, the self as political actor, the self as timekeeper, and so forth. Rock 'n' roll permeates the everyday lives of adults in American society. In commonsense terms, I examine what happened to the first, complete generation of rock 'n' roll fans—the baby boomer generation, now in late middle age and early old age. I argue that rock 'n' roll music continues to serve as a critical meaning resource for its adult fans as they continuously experience the becoming of self throughout life.

What about other styles of music, the skeptic might ask? Have baby boomers not graduated to other, more serene, perhaps more sophisticated, and, if you will, mellow styles of music? Have baby boomers not given up on loud music that is bad for one's failing hearing and on lyrics more relevant to the lives of their grandchildren? The answers to these plausible questions—and the heart of my argument—might be found in a recent article published in the "BBB," the baby boomers' bible: the weekly *AARP Webletter*. In the March 2, 2012, edition, Jacqueline Mitchard presented a list of popular songs that baby boomers should like. The follow-up article, published in May 15, 2012, humbled the author:

> Perhaps if Jacquelyn Mitchard's essay had been titled "My Favorite Songs: How Do They Compare to Yours?" (thanks for the suggestion, *Koalabelle*), we wouldn't have gotten so many angry comments and Facebook posts about our story, "16 Songs Everyone Over 50 Must Own."

Of course! Nobody, especially at our age, likes to be told what to do. So much for the power of music critics over baby boomers.

> But it wasn't only the headline that got readers riled up. People complained about everything from the pokiness of our website (we're working on it!) to the lack of songs with "Linda" in the title ("the name with the most songs written about it!!!," according to, you guessed it, Linda on Facebook).

Of course! People love and remember the songs directly relevant to their lives and selves, not those of the critics or experts.

> Mostly, though, Mitchard's greatest sin seemed to be that she left out the music you love—the music you listened to under the covers with a transistor radio, at a dance hall or a disco, in a dorm room with towels stuffed under the door, in a *Ford Mustang*, a hooch in Vietnam, or at a rally for peace or civil rights. As AARP community member *fishface33* says: "Songs are like pizza. We all have our favorite." And, for the most part, Mitchard failed to name that tune. . . .
>
> Sometimes it was a single song, like Fleetwood Mac's "Go Your Own Way" or Don McLean's "American Pie." Others regretted the absence of an artist (Bob Dylan was on many lists), a group (Crosby, Stills, Nash & Young is clearly a favorite, as is the Band, Cream, the *Grateful Dead*, the Police) or a style of music (Motown, by a mile).
>
> Mitchard couldn't win for losing. When she did pick a popular artist or group, like *the Beach Boys*, Beatles or Elvis, writers criticized her song choice. Her attempt to move things toward the twenty-first century (Coolio's "Gangsta's Paradise") was greeted with scorn ("Forget the disco and rap crap") equal only to that of those who expressed hostility or at least ambivalence about music from the more-distant past. *Madriver*'s note about this was wistful: "I'm over 50, but have to say you've captured some of the music my parents listened to. I'm not sure how I feel about that."

Of course! Baby boomers' kids were listening to Coolio. And, baby boomers' parents in general were not rock 'n' rollers.

> In fact, the upper end of the AARP demographic felt mostly left out, a sentiment voiced by *penstamon*. "Were the writer really concerned, there certainly would have been a 'Stardust' on the list (which is still considered the greatest song ever written), as well as an 'All the Things You Are,' etc. Maybe there would have even been room for a 'My Funny Valentine,' too. That would have been a nice touch."

Of course! These songs were popular among baby boomers' parents and especially grandparents.

> In your own lists, there were fewer mentions of *Bruce Springsteen* than we might have expected. The outraged musical theater fans mostly sat on the sidelines, and we didn't hear from a single reader lamenting the lack of *Louis Armstrong*, considered the father of jazz.

Of course! They were and remain rock 'n' rollers. Needless to say, the editors of the AARP newsletter used this story to remind the reader of its new AARP Internet radio:

> Listen to the new "Your Favorite Songs" channel on AARP InternetRadio, featuring reader picks. You spoke, we listened! (When the player opens, scroll to the right and you'll find it after "Modern Rock").

As Tia DeNora (2000: 62–63) so elegantly notes,

> music is a device or resource to which people turn in order to regulate themselves as aesthetic agents, as feeling, thinking and acting beings in their day-to-day lives. . . . Music can be used as a device for the reflexive process of remembering/constructing who one is, a technology for spinning the apparently continuous tale of who one is, the turning over of past experiences, for the cultivation of self-accountable imageries of the self.

SOCIOLOGICAL TAKES ON ROCK 'N' ROLL

We can trace sociological interest in rock 'n' roll at least as far as the conclusion of World War II. Four stages or moments in the sociological analysis of rock 'n' roll closely parallel the historical development of rock 'n' roll itself over the past sixty years. I briefly describe these four moments to shows their relevance to understanding adult experiences of this phenomenon.

The first moment of rock 'n' roll occurred during the 1950s, when the idea of *teenagers* emerged within general American culture and scholarly observers forged the concept of *youth culture* to explain this strange yet wondrous new population cohort. Whereas it is clear that cultural and musicological roots of rock 'n' roll can be traced back at least several decades (Friedlander 1996), the sociocultural impact of rock 'n' roll emerged after the conclusion of World War II.

Since its inception in the 1950s, rock 'n' roll has been associated with adolescents and has thus become a medium for both understanding and critiquing the adolescent generation. Some of the earliest sociological observers of rock 'n' roll focused on its positive functions for adolescent development. Talcott Parsons (1951), a major American social theorist, was interested in understanding the ways that the American family adjusted to changes taking place in the wider society following the war. Like other social observers, Parsons was aware of the emerging population bulge that was to be known as the baby boomer generation. The great increase in the birth rate resulted in rapid suburbanization, the expansion of mandatory high school education, and so forth. Parsons argued that the adolescent culture that emerged after World War II was a functional mechanism for the societal control of the energy of this burgeoning generation. He viewed American youth culture as a *secondary institution* that functioned as a *safety valve*. Through practices such as athletics and dances (read: rock 'n' roll), adolescents' potentially deviant activities (read: sex and aggression) are brought under the supervision of adults (206). Consider the prototypical 1950s and 1960s sock hop, where youngsters could learn how to relate to and interact with one another under the stern supervision of the adult *chaperone*. We have all heard tales of the good nuns who served as chaperones at Catholic school dances. They allowed you to touch your dance partner during a slow dance while enforcing safe distance with a ruler.

Parsons was also interested in the way that the family can support the personalities of its adult members through access to American youth culture. As Haralambos and Holborn (2008: 463) put it succinctly,

> adult personalities are also stabilized by the parents' role in the socialization process. This allows them to act out "childish" elements of their own personalities which they have retained from childhood but which cannot be indulged in adult society. For example, father is "kept on the rails" by playing with his son's train set. According to Parsons, therefore, the family provides a context in which husband and wife can express their childish whims, give and receive emotional support, recharge their batteries, and so stabilize their personalities.

Of course, Parsons based much, if not most, of his ideas about the family on the middle-class family as he knew it and as he grew up in it. He was not aware of the variations then and increasingly now in family structure and functioning as we know them. Nevertheless, he clearly provided a platform for analyzing the increasing and increasingly complex ways that adults use culture—rock 'n' roll music as well as toy train sets—to express their childhood whims and establish continuity between childhood and adulthood in their own lives.

James Coleman (1961) conducted a now classic survey of adolescent attitudes and behaviors in various northern Illinois communities in 1955.

Coleman was interested in studying the secondary school experience and adolescent status systems. He argued that teenagers used popular music to stratify, organize, and manage one another and that rock 'n' roll was a tool especially popular among working-class kids. Coleman found that rock 'n' roll was the most popular form of music among both boys and girls. Girls liked to listen to records or the radio more than boys, a phenomenon that Coleman explains with the observation that boys had a wider variety of leisure activities available to them. Nevertheless, both boys and girls used rock 'n' roll to learn prevailing values for gender roles. Girls used romantic ballads and fan club memberships to learn about boys, dating, and so forth. Boys used "less conventional" stars, such as Elvis Presley, to learn about adventure and masculinity. Overall, Coleman viewed rock 'n' roll positively, since "music and dancing provide a context within which (teen-agers) may more easily meet and enjoy the company of the opposite sex" (236). Many teenagers were "passionately devoted" to rock 'n' roll (315).

Researchers like Parsons and Coleman in fact wrote about baby boomers' older brothers and sisters. For many people born in the early 1940s, rock 'n' roll was a new style of music and musical culture to which they converted. Popular music in the 1950s, in terms of record and sheet music sales and radio play, was dominated by big band music (e.g., Lawrence Welk), lush orchestral music (e.g., Percy Faith), cabaret music (e.g., Judy Garland), and crooners (e.g., Frank Sinatra and Tony Bennett). Put differently, much of the music available to youth represented *adult culture* that was to be appreciated if one were to be successfully absorbed into adult society some day. The youth of the early 1950s were at the genesis of a distinctive *youth culture*.

The second moment of rock 'n' roll occurred during the mid-1960s through the 1970s. Rock 'n' roll music grew to become a cultural entity much greater than merely the beat for sock hops or the drive-in. It took on broader political implications through its links to the civil rights and antiwar movements. Sociologists such as Simon Frith (1981) and George Lewis (1983) conceptualized the second moment of rock 'n' roll as *popular culture*—the product of the popular culture industry in capitalistic society. They also acknowledged the fact that the rock 'n' roll audience was much more diverse than what the notion of "youth" implies. Experientially, there were white, black, gay, men's, and women's rock 'n' rolls and, subsequently, markets. Viewing rock 'n' roll music among adults as *popular culture* may be useful to the degree that the adult culture of rock 'n' roll reflects similar diversity. The marketing of rock 'n' roll to adults today also takes on the appearance of marketing strategies traditionally directed to youth—consider the great similarities between MTV and VH1.

The third moment of rock 'n' roll occurred in the 1970s and 1980s when rock 'n' roll lost some of its critical appeal and became increasingly entrenched in and controlled by the entertainment industry. The ensuing revolt against corporate rock 'n' roll, especially in terms of the new wave and punk movements in England, led British scholars such as Dick Hebdige (1979) and others from the Birmingham School to conceptualize rock 'n' roll as *subculture*. Subcultural theory denotes marginality and resistance to an authority, hegemonic or otherwise. The question I address later is whether rock 'n' roll can still function as a medium for political discourse for adults. The images of Bill Clinton jamming on a saxophone at an inauguration party or Barack Obama singing Reverend Al Green's "Let's Stay Together" makes the possibility of meaningful resistance among adult rock 'n' rollers problematic.

The fourth moment of rock 'n' roll began in the 1980s and extends through today. Sociologists have joined other scholarly observers to conceptualize rock 'n' roll simply as *culture* (e.g., Kaplan 1987). They saw rock 'n' roll as one feature of a postindustrial or postmodern culture undergoing radical transformation. The generational boundaries that so obviously delineated youth from their parents were cracking. Lawrence Grossberg (1992a), for example, proclaimed the death of rock 'n' roll insofar as it no longer functions to empower teenagers by differentiating them from their parents and other adults. By the 1990s, cross-generational—yet rock 'n' roll–inspired—pop music (e.g., Billy Joel and Madonna) that could be enjoyed by everyone had started to supplant rock 'n' roll as the dominant soundtrack in American culture. Rap music—also heavily inspired by rock 'n' roll—has helped diminish ethnic boundaries in pop music and has taken on much of rock 'n' roll's traditional political role. Yet, rock 'n' roll has not simply died. Rock 'n' roll acts of an earlier era continue to draw loyal audiences, while contemporary rock 'n' roll has dissolved into the pastiche of popular music that results in white rappers such as Eminem, rock and rapper groups such as Linkin Park, and pop acts such as Britney Spears, Beyonce, Justin Bieber, and their myriad of clones. Why, then, have so many adults not outgrown rock 'n' roll? The answer is that they refuse to stop growing. Sociologically, there are two concepts that can help us understand why and how they refuse to stop growing. The first is the *becoming of self*, derived from symbolic interactionist and existentialist notions of the experience of individuality. The second is *authenticity*, which serves as one of the key frameworks within which baby boomers make sense of their everyday life worlds through rock 'n' roll.

THE BECOMING OF SELF

The intellectual tradition of symbolic interactionism was founded on the idea of the self—who am I to myself. The social philosopher George Herbert Mead (1934) is generally thought to be the founder of interactionism. He strongly argued that the relationship between the individual and society was not mediated through genetics or personality but through the process of coming to oneself as a member of the community. The individual grows into adulthood and full membership in the community by developing a self based on meanings received from others.

Existential social thought later emerged to account for the fact that, in the post–World War II world, our sense of self is not simply fulfilled when we reach adulthood. Instead, the self is "a unique experience of being within the context of contemporary social conditions, an experience most notably marked by an incessant sense of becoming and an active participation in social change" (Kotarba 1984: 223). The incessant sense of becoming is a reflection of the contemporary need for the individual to be prepared to reshape meanings of self in response to the dictates of a rapidly changing social world. The well-integrated self accepts the reality of change and welcomes new ideas, new experiences, and reformulations of old ideas and experiences that help one adapt to change (Kotarba 1987).

The idea of *becoming* is one of the most important ideas in existentialist thought because it acknowledges responsibility for fashioning a self in the individual. Whereas Jean-Paul Sartre (1945) argued dramatically that we are condemned to be free and to choose who we are to become, Maurice Merleau-Ponty (1962) insisted more moderately and sociologically that we must ground our becoming of self in the real world to cope effectively with it. Thus, an effective strategy for becoming begins with a foundation of personal experience and the constraints of social structure while evolving in terms of the resources presented by culture. I argue that aging Americans work with a self originally assembled to some degree from the meanings provided by the rock 'n' roll idiom and that they continue to nurture the self within the ever-present cultural context of rock 'n' roll.

Jack Douglas (1984) notes that there are in fact two analytically distinct stages of becoming of self with which the modern actor contends. The first is the need to eliminate or control threats to the basic security of self (e.g., shame, meaninglessness, isolation from others, death). Although existential psychotherapists such as Yalom (1980) argue that chronic insecurity—or neurosis—is pervasive in our society, Douglas argues sociologically that it is more common for the sense of security to vary biographically, situationally, and developmentally. In general, adults try to shape everyday life experiences to avoid basic threats to the self. Basic threats to the adult self in our society would include divorce, the loss of a job, the loss of children (e.g., empty-nest syndrome), illness, disability, and poverty. The second stage of becoming of self involves growth of the sense of self. Growth occurs when the individual seeks new experiences as media for innovative and potentially rewarding meanings for self (Kotarba 1987). It is through growth—or self-actualization, as it is often referred to today—that life becomes rich, rewarding, full, and manageable.

Accordingly, adult fans nurture their interest in and experience with rock 'n' roll music for two reasons. On the one hand, keeping up with the music and culture that were so important to them when growing up helps them maintain continuity with the past and, thus, solidify the sense of self security. On the other, working hard to keep rock 'n' roll current and relevant to their lives helps adults grow as parents, as spiritual beings, and as friends.

The concept of the *existential self* tells us that the experience of individuality is never complete; the answer to the question "Who am I?" is always tentative. In the postmodern world, the mass media—including popular music—serve as increasingly important audiences to the self. The *self* is situational and mutable (Zurcher 1977). One can be various selves as the fast-paced, ever-changing, uncertain postmodern society requires.

In the chapters that follow, I inventory the ways that rock 'n' roll continues to affect the experiences of self among people raised on it. Since we experience multiple selves, the rock 'n' roll idiom contributes meaning to several or many of these selves.

AUTHENTICITY AND BABY BOOMER ROCK 'N' ROLLERS

Authenticity has long been a regular topic in both popular and professional discussions of popular music (Kotarba 2008, 2009). The popular music industry is concerned with two issues related to authenticity. The first is marketing and product definition. For example, Gigmasters is a nationwide agency that books musical acts (http://www.gigmasters.com). Among all the artists it promotes, groups that mimic the Rolling Stones are among the most popular. Gigmasters is very careful to indicate that its groups are not fakes that attempt to trick the audience into believing that they are really the Rolling Stones—they are touted as tribute bands. In one of its online ads, it notes,

> Satisfaction is exactly what fans of The Rolling Stones will get any time they view Rolling Stones tribute acts. That's because—from Mick's skinny bod to Keith's unkempt hair—Rolling Stones music played by cover groups sounds almost identical to that of the mega-rocker band.

This type of product definition and delineation has been a major attribute of all styles of popular music. As Richard Peterson (1997) has argued, the country music industry, centered in Nashville, Tennessee, became a powerful force in popular music by producing music that was marketed and appreciated as authentic country music.

Second, the mass media generate mountains of copy through stories on authenticity. Much of this material appears as critical evaluation of performers and performances in terms of authenticity. David Grazian (2003), in his work on blues music, writes at length about the importance that critics maintain in determining whether contemporary blues music and musicians are authentic. The mass media have field days over authenticity issues that are legal in scope—for example, the frequent court cases intended to establish which singing group has legal claim to the name "The Platters." They especially thrive on authenticity issues that are scandalous in tone—for example, the print mileage squeezed from the Milli Vanilli scandal in the early 1990s. I approach authenticity from a third perspective—that is, through the perceptions of middle-age and older fans in the pop music audience. The sociophilosophical field of phenomenology suggests strategies for studying experiences such as authenticity through fans' perspectives (Kotarba 2009).

PHENOMENOLOGY AND AUTHENTICITY

Phenomenological social theory focuses on the social contexts of consciousness (Freeman 1980). As Alfred Schutz (1967) argued, consciousness is made of practical knowledge that allows the person to navigate through everyday life. Practical knowledge allows the person to understand and even predict—take for granted, if you will—most events encountered in everyday life. Practical knowledge—or commonsense knowledge—is acquired simply and primarily through one's membership in a community. A community's common sense becomes its members' common sense. Objects and events are meaningful, or have meaning for us, after we actively make sense of them in concrete situations. Schutz (6) referred to this as *intentionality*—we intend or make sense of things because we are confronted by them and must make sense of them to control, protect, circumvent, and honor them. Yet, of all the things we encounter in everyday life, which ones do we choose to try to make sense of? Schutz (1964: 125) argued that this depends on the importance of the *purpose at hand*—that is, the situation in which we find ourselves. An object can be immediately relevant, absolutely irrelevant, or somewhere in between. In terms of the topic at hand, the need to assess the authenticity of a song, artist, or performance is likely to shift over time. I may possibly question whether REO Speedwagon today—with only one original member, Kevin Cronin—is the same REO Speedwagon that I listened to twenty years ago. Nevertheless, I engage that issue only when I must or when it has value for me to do so. For example, REO Speedwagon's authenticity is in my primary zone of relevance when I see the notice in the newspaper that it will perform in San Antonio next month and I have to decide whether I want to/should/must buy tickets and go.

Phenomenologists go one step further in their discussion of practical knowledge. Practical knowledge is couched in words, and *authenticity* is first and foremost a word. Words, both in our consciousness and in our interaction—or conversations—with others accomplish tasks for us. They do this through the powerful mechanism we call *reflexivity* (Garfinkel 1967). When we talk, our words not only describe something but also create a world in which that something can appear and is possible (Mehan and Wood 1975). On the one hand, musical authenticity is an idea or a linguistic/rationalistic device that people use to accomplish social interactional goals. The social situation largely determines when, how, and why an individual will involve the idea of *authenticity* or the word itself. On the other hand, musical authenticity is a social object that is cognitive in essence yet dealt with like any other feature of material objects (Mead 1934). Objects, like music performances, can be more or less authentic according to the meanings and evaluations we give them. Musical styles, too, can be authentic or inauthentic, and the assessment of either can be readily accomplished and justified by reference to the cultural rules governing authenticity.

Phenomenology tells us that although we take for granted the existence of authenticity as a feature of music and the "fact" that music can be more or less authentic or even inauthentic, we deal with authenticity as such only in situations in which authenticity can help us solve some other practical problem. Authenticity is therefore the product of intentional, reflexive, practical social interactions. Existential social thought, as we have seen, suggests that the most immediate and powerful practical problem is making sense of, fortifying, reconstructing, or saving our sense of self.

THE EXISTENTIAL SELF AND AUTHENTICITY

Existential social thought raises two issues related to my discussion of authenticity. First, we should expect that, in everyday life situations, authenticity is not experienced primarily as a variable. People do not ordinarily perceive music as more or less authentic. Instead, we should be open to the discovery and description of experiences in which music provides a sense of *authenticity or inauthenticity* to the self, as well as a resource for making sense of a particular situation. Put differently, inauthenticity could have positive uses in everyday life (see also Waskul 2009).

Second, the experience of inauthenticity, when dysfunctional for the self, may be akin to the notion of *alienation*. In existential thought, alienation refers to the experience of estrangement or distance from the world (Fontana 1980). This largely affective as well as rationalistic separation can result in a state of meaninglessness: if I depend on the world for meaning for my life but it is no longer available to me, then my sense of self is suddenly void. Propositionally, if I have filled my life over time with rock 'n' roll but realize that I no longer fit with rock 'n' roll, then I have a meaning void to fill.

By making claims of authenticity or inauthenticity in musical experiences, the individual simultaneously makes claims about the self. I have elsewhere referred to these claims as *authenticity work* in everyday life among baby boomers (Kotarba 2009). I define authenticity work as the interactional process by which the assessment of authenticity in cultural phenomena, such as popular music, serves as a resource or tool for recreating, defining, verifying, or developing a viable self. This viable self may or may not necessarily be perceived as authentic in so many words. There are many styles or depictions of self that can be the outcome of *authenticity work*. The point is that *authenticity work* creates a relationship between music and the self that can be positive or negative on the self and that can lead to stagnation or growth.

ROCK MUSIC AND THE EXPERIENCE OF AUTHENTICITY IN MIDDLE AGE—AND BEYOND

Critics and fans alike have traditionally viewed popular music, especially in terms of its rock 'n' roll iterations, as a meaning resource for youth navigating through adolescence. I explore instead the relevance of popular music for self-identity through middle age and beyond. As noted, existential social thought tells us that the process of self-development is constant throughout life. What changes are life circumstances, the biological and affective aging process, reassessment of the past, and strategic relationships with others. As these contingencies change, so does the experience of self. As Andrea Fontana (1976) notes, the activities used during adulthood to make sense of the self are likely to be the same types of activities used to make sense of getting old. The baby boomer generation was the first Western generation to grow up entirely in the world of rock 'n' roll music and culture, and many baby boomers experienced rock 'n' roll as a master script for life. Therefore, this highly self-integrated cultural resource, enhanced by the power of the popular media, remains central to the self-identity of many baby boomers as they approach old age.

The issue of authenticity can appear in any number of pop music experiences. The starting point for this analysis is the argument that, in our postmodern world, we experience different selves in different situations and different social worlds (Zurcher 1977). Music can affect any or all of these selves in different ways and at different times. I examine the ways that authenticity work fits the eleven selves relevant to the rock 'n' roll experience.

ON WITH OUR JOURNEY . . .

A sociological approach to any phenomenon seeks to illustrate and analyze trends, patterns, and changes over time. Given this protocol, the
experience of rock 'n' roll music and culture varies among adults by
gender, social class, ethnicity, educations, and all the other classic sociological variables. I try to account for as much variation as needed to
understand the rock 'n' roll experience, but I ask the reader to substitute
his or her own rock 'n' roll biography to make personal sense of the
conceptual argument that I am making. Perhaps as important, I ask the
reader to conceive of other models of the self experienced, survived, cele-
brated, or regretted from that rock 'n' roll biography.

TWO

The E-Self: iTunes and Satellite Radio

As the rock 'n' roll fan ages, many of the attractive aspects of the earlier self are more difficult to maintain. There is a tendency for youthfulness, energy, risk taking, appearance, sensuality, and other aspects of the adolescent or young adult self to become either less available or less desirable. Our culture does, however, provide a self-identity that resonates with the affluence of middle age as well as with the continuing need to establish status/self-esteem. The *e-self* refers to an experience of individuality in which the affective and philosophical self-resources of rock 'n' roll media are displaced or at least supplemented by the increasingly technological and commodified aspects of the media. For the aging fan, what you play your music on can be at least as, if not more, important than what you play.

Middle age results in less concert attendance and more music experience in the comfort of home and automobile and, for the energetic, on the jogging trail. A content analysis of *Wired* magazine (June 2012), which is geared toward the affluent and technologically interested adult, discloses the strategy of marketing rock 'n' roll to its audience. There are ads for Harmon Kardon high-performance headphones for "perfect sound by design"; HP Spectre ultrabook computer to "hear your favorite song for the first time" ApogeeMic studio quality microphone for iPad, iPhone, and Mac; and the Proclaim DMT-100 integrated speaker system at a price of \$25,995 to "rock your Amadeus." The traditional ads for iPods and other MP3 players have been increasingly supplanted by numerous ads and reviews of smartphones that do it all and cloud systems in which to store all your music while making it available to play on your iPhone, iPad, and Mac.

Such marketing resonates with the adults it targets. George is a fifty-eight-year-old Anglo electrical engineer who just installed a satellite radio system in his Lexus sedan. He sees two benefits of his musical purchase: "I don't have to mess with CDs or radio anymore. I get to play only the music I like to hear. . . . There are stations dedicated just to '80s heavy metal. Cool." George has also effectively eliminated the hassles of concert crowds and debates over musical tastes with peers. High technology puts his e-self in control of his musical environment. George can experience his music with the aura of cultural independence that affluent adults seek.

Electronics companies are very aware of the economic power of the baby boomer consumer. According to the Consumer Electronics Association, US sales of consumer electronics jumped 16 percent to $186.4 billion in 2011, from $156.5 billion in 2006. In terms of music-related commodities, sales of MP3 players, including the incredibly popular Apple iPod, jumped dramatically to $3.8 billion in 2005 from $1.1 billion in 2004 (Wingfield and Clark 2006).

Baby boomers account for approximately 55 percent of all iPod purchases. Just about every baby boomer in our society has access to the Internet—whether at work, home, or the public library. These two technological phenomena provide not only a convenient way to listen to music but also a mechanism for helping the rock 'n' roller become a *music manager* and a *music friend*. Tom is a sixty-two-year-old manager of an oil-drilling supply company. His wife bought an iPod for him for Christmas 2008. She and his two teenage children have told him repeatedly that he should have an iPod because he was such a music fan:

> Ever since the iPod came out, in 2003 I believe, my people kept asking me if I wanted one. I kept telling them no. I like to listen to the radio and, besides, I really do not have that many songs to download. I have a CD player that I don't use much the way it is.

As Tom's friends at work and in the neighborhood bought their iPods or received them as gifts, he started to see them in a new light. Part of his interest was peer pressure; that is, he did not want to be the last guy to get an iPod. But a more forceful reason was Tom's interest in managing his music. When cassette tapes were a popular medium in the 1970s, Tom would type up and maintain a catalog list of all his tapes. When he obtained his first personal computer in the early 1980s—an IBM 8086, he recalls—he put this list on a disk. Tom recently concluded that an iPod would actually let him locate all his music in a convenient and usable place: "I know, I have quite a bit of music on my hard drive, but I really do not listen to much of it. I might as well play a CD if I'm tied to my PC that way."

Tom hinted quite explicitly that he wanted an iPod for Christmas, but he took his wife to the Apple store in the mall to make sure that she purchased the correct model. Santa Claus came through, and the pretty black iPod left under the tree has become Tom's hobby—or obsession? His iPod has made him a listener again, not just a musical bookkeeper:

> I was thinking just the other day about how much the iPod is like an old-fashioned transistor radio. I take my iPod with me everywhere I go, like a radio. My iPod has all my favorite music on it. . . . Our transistors had all our music, too. . . . The Top 40 was our music, remember? Now, I have to really hunt around to find music I want to listen to on the radio, and I usually come up short.

His iPod also helps him be a better *music friend*. Like many baby boomers, Tom uses shared music as a medium for maintaining friendships. Whether buddies from the old neighborhood, former dorm mates from college, current colleagues at work, or partners from the gym, they all tend to be music fans; that is, music seems to be the one link across situations and time. Needless to say, they do not get out to see live music as much as they used to or would ideally like to. Sharing music fills the bill; iPods are a great way to share:

> We used to share songs by burning CDs. The problem with that was someone had to buy the whole CD and burn it to a CD to give it to you, or burn it to a hard drive to send it by email. Now, you only have to buy the songs you want and you only send a song or two to your buddy.

Ironically, the iPod has allowed baby boomers to return to the old world of rock 'n' roll in which they grew up, where "singles" ruled the land.

Sharing music enhances friendships three ways. First, shared music gives friends something to talk about besides work, sports, families, health, and so forth. Music is a very personal topic that is important to talk about because it is a fun topic. Music becomes, in the word of Carlos Castaneda (1971), a *separate reality* beyond the mundane world of work sports, families, and health. Second, shared music gives friends a link to the past. To send an old Led Zeppelin song to a friend via the Internet is a comfortable way to deal with the past without reducing the past to mere nostalgia. The Led Zeppelin song is contemporary because it exists online, in the iPod, and in one's ear buds when listening to the song on the way to work. Third, shared music is a simple way to maintain friendships. There is little risk of communicating an issue that could be questioned, raise controversy, or be misunderstood. Van Morrison is Van Morrison and will always be Van Morrison to Van's fans.

Finally, although much of the baby boomer's everyday sources of information are online, one may still read newspapers and magazines to keep up with the world—but in a contemporary way. Take the *Wall Street Journal*, for example. Its editors know their readership perhaps better than any other new source. While market news is the raison d'être for the *WSJ*—the voice of capitalism—the readers are not your father's typical pocket watch–wearing and cigar-chomping robber barons. The *WSJ* section "Pursuits" on February 18, 2006, comments on the music playing on Winter Olympic iPods (2):

> Skeleton: System of a Down Skeleton racer Chris Soule mostly listens to this heavy-metal band right before a race to "find a rhythm that gets me throughout a section of the track," he says. The music "stays in the back o my mind, a tool I use as I prepare myself."
>
> Bobsled: Metallica Bobsledder Steve Mesler turns to heavy rock like Metallica, Rage Against the Machine and Oomph, a German band. "This helps me get more amped up for competition," he says. "In bobsled, the push athlete's job is to go crazy for five seconds and then or job is pretty much done."

A quick perusal of more recent *WSJ* sections—"Pursuits," "Personal Journal," and "Weekend Journal"—reveals articles on singer-songwriter Tori Amos's favorite rock videos, popular consumer electronic devices, and a review of singer-songwriter Neil Young's concert documentary *Neil Young: Heart of Gold*.

AARP RADIO: BLUE-HAIRED ROCKERS

As we have seen, several features of everyday life converge to shape the aging rock'n'roller's musical experience: computers, the Internet, getting older, and consistent interest in music. The most relevant media may already be the computer and the Internet. Thus, it is not surprising that one of the single most relevant, everyday life sources of meaning for politics, consumerism, health, relationships, and leisure for the aging rocker, either in or approaching retirement, is the AARP. The American Association of Retired People is self-described as ". . . a nonprofit, nonpartisan membership organization for people age 50 and over" (AARP 2011). For $16 a year, one gains access to all sorts of information and services that are increasingly published on-line. The AARP has very recently entered the world of popular music programming to take advantage of the access it has to and reputation it has among senior citizens.

The AARPs began offering its Internet radio service in June 2011. The service is free for members, who must be over the age of 50 to belong. The Concord Music Group, an independent record company, programs 18 channels for AARP. The player is linked to AARP's site, and its design was kept simple for ease of navigation, with buttons only for playing and pausing a song, and skipping ahead to the next one. The channels will each have about 500 songs in rotation. The marketing strategy at AARP is to attract those baby boomers who still love their music but are not sure where and how to locate it in the digital age. The costs of AARP's service will be paid through advertising. AARP and Concord will share any profits.

In an interview with Marc Morgenstern, Concord's chief market and asset development officer, Robert Sisario of the *New York Times* asked whether the goal was to mix new music with the old: "Older people get a bum rap, that they're kind of frozen in time. . . . Everyone has a certain affinity for the music of their youth," he added. "But people really do want to find something new, something that may not stray far from what they're familiar with but bring a huge gust of fresh air" (Sisario 2011).

I'm betting my money that the AARP digital music programming will be a big success. The progenitor of this type of programming, Pandora, is already a very successful alternative to broadcast radio. Sociologically, we should expect the popularity of the AARP music programming to be fueled to a large extent by the fact that it is an AARP project. The aging rock 'n' roller learned one big lesson from middle age: what gadget you play your music on can be at least as, if not more important, to your sense of self than what particular style of music you play. Put differently, media developments like the AARP music programming may serve to unify the otherwise fragmenting music audience by making the shopping experience the most self-rewarding part of the whole enterprise thing for the aging rocker. We will see.

THREE

The Intimate Self

A significant aspect of the historical popularity of rock 'n' roll music is its value in helping us make sense of intimate relationships and romantic others. Thomas Scheff, in his *What Does Love Have to Do with It?* (2011), explores the meaning of the pop love song. In interpreting eighty years of pop love song lyrics, Scheff sees four types of lyrics: heartbreak, infatuation, love, and other. The proportions of each type are rather stable over time, in spite of changes in musical styles and our culture more generally. As much as we all love love songs, Scheff's conclusion is rather sad: popular love songs tend to steer listeners away from a healthier view of emotions surrounding love. The English language is simply not suited to relaying emotions and instead suppresses rather than acknowledges emotions. Equally critical is the strategy of examining rock 'n' roll to read song lyrics objectively and conclude that they can be quite sexist and put women at a disparaging disadvantage (e.g., McRobbie 1978).

I see rock 'n' roll as a bit more friendly than these critics do. Although there may be truth in their arguments, their evidence rests on the assumption that lyrics have intrinsic meanings that subsequently cause listeners to think and ultimately behave in certain ways. Following the symbolic interactionist and phenomenological traditions, I argue that song lyrics—including rock 'n' roll lyrics—display an open-ended horizon of meaning for their audiences. What a music performance means is largely a function of the situation in which it is experienced and the particular self needs of the audience member (Kotarba 1994b).

An example is the *our song* phenomenon. An our song is one used to define—rationally as well as affectively—a relationship. In discussing our songs in my popular music courses, I have often asked students to talk about their our songs. I never cease to be amazed at the wide—and I mean *wide*—range of songs used as love songs. I have had students who have chosen hard-core punk songs, such as the Ramones' "Pinhead" and the Stooges' "I Wanna Be Your Dog," to be performed at their weddings. As time passes, the rock 'n' roll audience matures, biographies evolve, men's and women's relationships change, popular music commodities come and go, and cultural themes available through the media advance. Thus, we can expect the actual lived experience of popular music to change among baby boomers.

Our songs are clearly not limited to baby boomers. Preadolescents, for example, commonly choose songs that remind them of a boy or a girl, but these kids are often too shy to disclose this fact to the other! For mature rock 'n' roll fans, the our song can function at least two ways. First, it provides meaning for benchmark events in the relationship. Shirley is a fifty-four-year-old Latina salesperson who is a big Los Lobos fan. She builds anniversary activities around one particular song that she and her husband both enjoy:

> We fell in love with "Nadie Quiere Sufrir" at a Los Lobos concert when we were still just dating. It is a very pretty waltz that actually comes from an Edith Piaf song. . . . I make sure the CD [with the song] is in the car when we drive to [our anniversary] dinner. He bought me the CD for our anniversary a few years ago. . . . Oh, I guess it just makes us feel young again.

Second, the our song can help the person feel like a lover. As couples age and perhaps find themselves feeling and acting less romantic over time, the our song can function as a quick fix. Rob is a fifty-eight-year-old Anglo executive who has maintained a serious relationship with Tommy, a forty-seven-year-old artist, for about fifteen years. Their song is Queen's "Bohemian Rhapsody":

> There will never be another Freddie Mercury. It was really special to have our own gay rock icon. . . . I surprise Tommy by playing "Bohemian Rhapsody" now and again. Tommy is still thrilled that I remember it. . . . Why? Well, it's one of those songs that make you feel good, to feel that you can be gay and a rocker at the same time. . . . I like doing things for Tommy. We are just so busy with our careers—makes us feel like an old married couple!

Needless to say, the rock 'n' roll industry is aware of the market here for its goods and services among baby boomers. One of the more recent examples is the advent and growing popularity of rock 'n' roll cruises. Carnival Cruise Lines offers the following "Rock 'n' roll Cruise Vacation" in an online ad:

> What could be cooler than a seven-day Caribbean cruise with legendary big-hair 1970s/80s rockers Journey, Styx and REO Speedwagon? Well . . . we'll reserve comment. But, if your idea of a totally awesome vacation is a seven-day cruise with legendary big-hair 1970s/80s rockers Journey, Kansas, Styx and REO Speedwagon, you're in luck.

Baby boomers use rock 'n' roll materials for a range of romantic purposes. They use music as birthday and Christmas gifts (e.g., CDs and iTunes gift cards). They use music to help them appreciate other media, such as films and television. It's somewhat amazing how the theme song from *Seinfeld* can trigger nostalgic and romantic feelings, simply because a couple shared their love of the *Seinfeld* television program when they first started going out.

FIVE SONGS ABOUT WOMEN

Romantic experiences are very important to baby boomers. Although we commonly associate baby boomers with hard rock, protest music, and even disco, we must recall that growing up in the 1960s and 1970s was as romantic as any other youthful period in modern history. As much as FM radio indexed events in the world around us back then, pop versions of rock 'n' roll were still very much present on AM radio and even television. I remember religiously watching the *Glen Campbell Goodtime Hour* on CBS in 1967 and 1968 in the evening when I spent the summer at home in Chicago as a college student at Illinois State University. Like most of my friends who did not have to go to Vietnam, we worked hard during the day in any number of old factories, putting in as much overtime as possible to be able to live well in the fall when we returned to school. (I had a great job, cleaning spilt oil on the floor around machine presses that punched out aluminum beer cans. I made a robust $3.35 an hour, thanks to the then all-powerful steelworkers union.)

But for one evening a week, I escaped the working-class industrialized south side to listen to country singers make sense of my urban life. Glen Campbell was one of the new breed of country pop musicians becoming known as singer-songwriters. A singer-songwriter was something like a folk singer but not as dreary, old, or consequential. Glen Campbell, with his blond hair over his ears, was no Bob Dylan, but that was OK. Glen sang country pop songs that fit the times—he sang songs about women. The lyrics, though, for those of us who were college boys, were accessible versions of the otherwise droll poems we learned about—no, memorized—in freshman lit. The best songs in the Glen Campbell era were written and performed by a gentle man whose name was John Hartford. His best song was "Gentle on My Mind," made popular by Campbell. The song was a sweet story of a free-spirited young man who was a model for those twenty-year-olds who wanted to own freedom but not without a woman to be somewhere on the horizon:

> And it's knowin' I'm not shackled
> By forgotten words and bonds

It was kind of a prerelationship song for young men who truly, if naively,
believed that relationships can exist without nurturing, exchanging, sharing, and so on.

> That keeps you in the back roads by the rivers of my memory
> That keeps you ever gentle on my mind

Romantic musical experiences happen two ways. First, fans can interpret
(or reinterpret) music to fit romantic needs. As we will see, the meaning
of a song can change as the relationship changes. If the music fan needs
or wants a positive message about the other, he or she will find it. Second, fans can gravitate toward music that can be perceived as romantic.
Autobiographically, "Smokey" Bill Robinson and the Miracles' "Tracks of
My Tears" was a constant play on my 45 record player in 1966 when it
applied comforting words to yet another heartbreak in my life. My guess
is that I would not have been drawn as much to this new record if I did
not have a personal need for its plaintive prose. In general, fans gravitate
toward music that fits their everyday life concerns.

The main point here is that rock 'n' roll music works because the
experience that it produces is *dramatic*. Rock 'n' roll allowed me to experience romance in the same ways that movie stars, TV characters, and
characters in literature experience it. There can be no other explanation
for the overwhelming and consistent popularity of popular music. It does
something powerful for the listener, beyond the power of the lyrics.

Two scholarly traditions offer strong suggestions for a discussion of
the power of romantic pop music. Cultural studies scholars have strongly
argued that any meaningful examination of society and social processes
requires a serious critique of private and public structures of meanings
(Carey 1989). Traditional approaches to the study of culture, which see it
as a distinguishable product of institutional processes (e.g., Gans 1974),
are being replaced by current efforts to conceptualize culture as pervasive in all social life. The postmodernist project, in particular, has forged a
model of cultural studies that posits the sociological observer as a cultural critic whose objective is the disclosure of ideological, aesthetic, political, economic, sexist, and other themes in cultural phenomena, as well as
the critical examination of the production (i.e., logic and devices) of cultural phenomena (Hall 1980). Cultural studies encourage a holistic and
literary appreciation of cultural phenomena as *text*, including the dramatic and romantic features of rock 'n' roll.

A symbolic interactionist approach looks at the relationship between
lived experience and the cultural resources available to the actor to make
sense of that experience. Denzin's (1989, 82) interpretive interactionism
project, for example, focuses on the epiphanic moments or the dramatic
life experiences "which radically alter and shape the meanings which
people assign to themselves and their life projects." As personal troubles
become public issues (e.g., in terms of given through formal or informal

interaction), they acquire cultural meanings. Yet, given the constancy of everyday life, we should expect biography and culture to intersect in observable ways in situations both more mundane and perhaps more positive than those signified by the term *crisis*. For example, fundamental meanings for everyday life can emerge during joyful or even ascetic experiences, such as the creative moments in art, music performance, or music appreciation (Kotarba 1984).

Culture works because it can affect all facets and features of our existence. Culture is not simply a rational assessment of beauty or a proximate statement of truth. Culture of all kinds affects us totally. Consequently, culture can work the same way in different genres. My experience of "Gentle on My Mind" or any of the songs that follow is/can be as romantic, heart-throbbing, sad, joyful, depressing, or cool as any scene from *Gone with the Wind* or a movement from Beethoven's Fifth. Music can make our otherwise mundane lives dramatic. Pop music makes this magical experience possible for all of us—what a great gift!

In the remainder of this chapter, I discuss the meaning use of rock 'n' roll music as a critical component of adult culture.[2] Conceptually, I examine popular music in general as a cultural form that is a very important source of meaning for its audiences. Popular music allows us to see both mundane and dramatic experiences of meaning use. Popular music allows us to see the historical transformation of a cultural form from modern to postmodern, for example, in the ways that popular music acquired a cinemagraphic dimension in recent years (e.g., MTV, VH1, BET). I focus on my reading of popular music as an audience member, not as a critic who can independently arrive at the cultural significance of a phenomenon. Although the present reader may argue that I could not realistically separate the two viewpoints, my approach is in tune with current thinking in sociology that analysis is always produced within and affected by the writer's biographical and theoretical stance (Johnson 1975).

I have chosen to examine the male experience of rock 'n' roll music to counter an overly simplistic argument in the literature on gender and rock music mentioned earlier. The argument is commonly made that rock music is sexist because it (1) contains lyrics that are sexist, (2) supports— implicitly and explicitly—an adolescent male culture that is repressive to women, and (3) prohibits the active and equal involvement of women in the creation and performance of rock music (e.g., McRobbie 1978). Rock 'n' roll music is noteworthy among contemporary cultural forms because it displays a wide, open-ended horizon of meaning for its audiences. What a rock music performance means is largely a function of the situation in which it is entertained and the particular self needs of the audience member (Kotarba 1994b). While it is clear that rock music can present messages interpreted as sexist, it is also true that rock music presents messages that can be used more congenially. The gender-related meanings of rock music, especially in terms of the types of performances sought by a particular audience member, vary biographically. As men's relationships with women change, popular musical commodities come and go, and cultural themes available through the media evolve, we expect the actual lived experience of popular music to change. Romance comes in different colors and shapes.

MY SONGS

If you ask, rock 'n' roll fans have no trouble telling you what their favorite songs are. I routinely assign the students in my Sociology of Popular Music course to interview long-term rock 'n' roll fans, usually aging baby boomers who grew up with rock 'n' roll, and to ask them this question. Respondents typically come up with songs that are connected, at least by memory, to specific events and people in their past. Most married respondents, for example, can cite an our song that served to define, solidify, or bond their relationships with their spouses. Men love to talk about songs that "remind them" of the important women in their lives.

When I think about my favorite songs over a career as a rock 'n' roller spanning more than fifty years, I am struck by how many of them are about women. I am especially surprised when I recall that I grew up in and lived through historical periods in which songs about war, peace, cars, the beach, drugs, and nothing (e.g., rock and orchestral instrumentals such as "Rebel Rouser" by Dwayne Eddie and "Theme from a Summer Place" by Percy Faith) were very popular.

I can think of five songs in particular that have helped me considerably when women or a particular woman was a great mystery to me—which, I confess, has been most of my life. These songs all frame women in a romanticized, thus pleasurable, view. For biographical reasons perhaps too complex to go into now (e.g., being raised Catholic and placing women on an unrealistically lofty moral pedestal), I never liked songs that were overtly mean or degrading to women. The Rolling Stones' "Under My Thumb," which was a great hit with most of my male friends back in college, comes to mind. I discuss my lived experience of each song in the following terms:

- the artist who performed the song,
- the situation in which the song was relevant (e.g., occasion, time, and location),
- the nature of the woman in question (e.g., real or ideal),
- the meaning of the woman/women in general derived from the song,
- the response of others in my life to the song, and
- the medium presenting the song to the situation in question.

I am discussing these songs in chronological order. I am not suggesting that any one of them has been more important to me than the others.

"Runaround Sue": Dion Dimucci

I was in eighth grade at St. Turibius School in Chicago in 1960. In efforts to construct role models and peer status for ourselves, my male friends and I all had our favorite singers. We measured singers on the basis of overall coolness, cool hair, and music. Pompadours were de rigueur. Bobby liked Rick Nelson. Bobby Darin belonged to my buddy Matt. Bobby Rydell was OK, but Frankie Avalon and Neil Sedaka were not all that cool . . . maybe because girls liked them a little too much. Everybody knew that Dion was my man. His hair was great, with two rolls on each side of his head ready to cascade down his forehead at any time. He was Italian, which was a good predictor of good looks. I could be trusted to bring all of Dion's 45 singles to the basement dance parties held just about every Friday evening in the old neighborhood.

I was familiar with, and liked, Dion's earlier doo-wop work with his backup group, the Belmonts. But "Runaround Sue" was special. It sounded virtually a cappella, with a touch of plaintive alto sax at the end. Dion sang about someone and something new to a thirteen-year-old kid: a bad girl. And, he sang hurt. I was in love with a real Sue myself back then: Suzy B. Suzy was the perfect thirteen-year-old woman, about seventy pounds of skinny perfection with white blond hair. I was the perfect nerd. My one "date" with Suzy, if you can call it that, occurred when my buddy Danny Lindsey (a really big Elvis fan) and I met Suzy at Sharon Heath's house to share a six-pack of NeHi sodas in the basement. Did I ever kiss Suzy? Give me a break. I held her hand that evening for about ten minutes, terrified that the nervous sweat flowing from my hand would wash her hand away. But I did buy her a gift: a copy of Sheb Wooley's "Purple People Eater," which I slipped her one day as we passed through the hall between classes. I do not think I ever said more than thirty words to her, let alone "I like you."

When DJ Dick Biondi started playing "Runaround Sue" on WLS radio in Chicago, I thought it was an omen from God. Hearing a namesake song on the radio about one's girlfriend was too much to ask for. Perhaps that explains why name songs were so popular in the 1950s and early 1960s. I was oblivious to the literal, ominous meaning of the lyrics. I spent numerous Saturday evenings on my bicycle, roaming around from friends' houses to the park to the candy store, waiting for the "Wild I-tralian" to play my song. (I clearly was incapable of generating an inter-actionally consensual "our song" with Suzy!) I grasped my little six-transistor, nine-volt portable radio (which just about everyone had by this point in the history of electronic media) in my hand. When those first few scat sounds came over the speaker, I thought my bicycle would be pulled into the sky like some kind of south side Mary Poppins.

Pan ahead several weeks, past eighth-grade graduation, to the Junior Holy Name Society Summer Dance in the basement church hall. I heard from one of her girlfriends that Suzy would be there, and I looked forward to seeing her, dancing with her, and maybe even telling her I liked her. When I saw her walk down the stairs from the street, I about died. She was with an older guy (sixteen or seventeen, maybe?) who looked like Dion—Italian, great black hair, cool, and so forth. I might as well have been dead for all the attention Suzy gave me. When the dance DJ played "Runaround Sue," it took on a whole different meaning. For the first time, I really heard the words and shared in Dion's hurt: "I should have known from the very start / This girl would leave me with a broken heart." But the warning to other boys was clear: "So if you don't want to cry like I do / Stay away from Runaround Sue."

I knew that Suzy B. really wasn't a bad girl, even though glib moral judgments were a feature of being raised in a conservative culture in those days, a readily available method for making sense of an adolescent's increasingly complex and mystifying world. Nevertheless, the song allowed me to share responsibility for my sadness with the idealized Suzy. I didn't feel bad simply because I was a failure but also because "she goes out with all the guys."

Pan ahead to 1986. I was back in Chicago for our twenty-fifth grammar school reunion. We were all there, at the Black Knight Hall on Pulaski Road, all looking very thirty something. The DJ played it, obviously not as my song but merely as another oldie but goodie that night. I felt a little bit of tingle. Suzy and I talked quite a bit that evening, swapping hip stories about our kids and our spouses. I danced one dance with Suzy, a slow dance to Elvis's "I Can't Help Falling in Love." (Danny Lindsey was in heaven!) While we were dancing, Suzy laughingly told me that she really liked me back in eighth grade but was much too bashful to ever tell me. When I got back to Houston, I sent her flowers, with the simple and final message: "Thanks for being Suzy B."

Pan ahead again to 2008. I conducted a brief telephone interview with Dion to update my understanding of his music and career. In a very laid-back way—which he attributes to his semiretirement to Boca Raton, Florida—he noted that he spent a good part of his leisure time talking to men's groups, including local Catholic organizations such as Holy Name Societies and the Knights of Columbus. He relates his biography and how his Catholic faith was a source of strength that helped him eventually conquer serious drug dependency as a young man growing up in the Bronx, New York, and embarking on a very successful music career. His faith also helped him stay married to one woman, his one love of life, whom he met back in the Bronx.[3]

"Sweet Thing": Van Morrison

It's 1971. I'm back in Chicago, this time as a special education teacher in the public schools. My personal commitment to educably retarded kids was buttressed by the draft deferment that the job afforded me. I was living at home with my parents, making a fairly good salary with little overhead and spending most of my free time in the bar. Life was still one big question mark. Women were still a great mystery to me and my other single draft-dodging buddies. (Our friends in the army seemed better able to make sense of women. They had the Guess Who's "American Woman" to help them cope with relationships mangled, if not destroyed, by the separation and stress of war.) We had college educations and good jobs, but it seemed like all the women in the clubs still liked guys who looked like Frankie Avalon. Conventional moralistic strategies for interpreting women, such as "good girl" and "bad girl," which had some currency through high school and into college, were simply useless now. Remember, we were the generation of men who went from "Runaround Sue" to sexually liberated Earth Mothers in the course of a very few years. We also experienced the highs and the lows of different kinds of relationships. All bets were off on women.

I encountered "Sweet Thing" one pleasant spring evening in the bar where my boys and I hung out because it sponsored our bowling team. I was with two friends. We smoked a great joint before we entered the bar, rolled with some "killer weed" brought back from 'Nam by a returning and surviving buddy/hero. I was at the bar, sucking on a bourbon and water, when someone played "Sweet Thing" on the jukebox. I had never heard "Sweet Thing" before because it was the B-side song on a 45 record—the A-side song was the very popular "Moondance." "Sweet Thing" begins with an energetic acoustic guitar that simply builds up speed as the song progresses. I could not quite understand much of the lyrics, but I knew, I could feel, that Van Morrison was singing about a woman. He never described her and I never saw her, but she was there.

I bought the album that "Sweet Thing" was on, a now-classic work called *Astral Weeks*. "Sweet Thing" was one of those album songs that was officially seven minutes long but seemed to last a day when listened to after a joint. I listened to it constantly. I dubbed a copy to play on the new cassette player that I had bought for my car. (Oldies freaks and top-40 types were still buying eight tracks, but those of us in the know knew better.)

Although Van Morrison was singing to a woman, albeit an idealized woman, the message I got from the song was not about women at all. It was about me. The great joy I received from "Sweet Thing" was a glimpse of the feelings that I would have when I finally found *my* woman. Van was describing the person that I wanted to be when I found her. He was preparing me for her, teaching me the mature lesson that perfection is the result of my work, my commitment. A woman could only share in my perfection, not give it to me. The climax of the song, both musically and affectively, is ascetic (giving) rather than sensual (taking): "I will reach my hands into the night time sky / And touch a star that shines in your eye."

Van Morrison fans are now aging men. Women don't tune into him as much, and I'm not sure why. Van Morrison is a spiritual experience for most fans, not a source of meaning about women as he has been for me. He provides a mechanism for bonding among his male fans, as witnessed by the constant sharing of dubbed tapes and CDs. A very nice and fashionable Christmas gift for an elderly, middle-class Van Morrison fan for several years now has been a boxed CD set of the best of Van Morrison. Increasingly, this preferred gift has been a boxed DVD set of recent Van Morrison concerts. This is the kind of gift that a thoughtful wife gives such a man, knowing without hesitation that she probably won't share the music with him, but that's OK. A smart wife knows that the woman alluded to in "Sweet Thing" is her.

Pan ahead to September 2006. I attended my first Austin City Limits music festival. My wife Polly and I drove up to Austin specifically to attend the Van Morrison performance. Van does not perform often in Texas, so this was a real treat for a big fan like me. The crowd in Zilker Park on Ladybird Lake was huge. The evening was warm yet lively due to the seemingly constant breeze in the Hill Country. The crowd was clearly a bit older than the fans attending the Deadboy and the Elephantmen, the Kings of Leon, or the I Love You but I've Chosen Darkness performances at Austin City Limits. We arrived about one hour before the sunset start time and had to walk around a bit to find a spot to park our lawn chairs. In fact, the area in front of the main stage was a virtual sea of lawn chairs—these old rock 'n' rollers certainly know how to do things comfortably. The freaky thing was that everyone looked like we looked. The men were in their late fifties or sixties, looking very upper-middle class with their neatly pressed carpenter shorts and nice leather sandals. Most had a bit of a tummy but were sufficiently hip to know to wear new or recent Van Morrison T-shirts that fit better than the ones they bought in 1968. There were a lot more wives present now than in 1968.

Van led a fabulous large band, and he played a bit more saxophone than usual. He was backed on vocals by two marvelous singers. He did not sing "Sweet Thing" that wonderful evening, but all the sweet things in the audience wisely looked away when their men were kindly offered and took a hit on the one joint that seemingly circulated throughout the crowd.

"Come Saturday Morning": The Sandpipers

It's 1974, and I'm sitting in a movie theater with my fiancée in Kansas City, watching Liza Minnelli's film debut *The Sterile Cuckoo*. I don't recall exactly what the film said to me about women or life in mid-decade, but I certainly remember the soundtrack song. "Come Saturday Morning" is a lovely pop tune, highly orchestrated and sung by a studio male vocal group never heard from again. I have always had a weakness for pretty pop songs, much to the chagrin of my male friends who gravitated solely toward hard rock or the blues. This song seemed to fit—my life, the film, my feelings about the woman soon to become my wife, as well as my wimpy taste in music. Life was peaceful. The war was over, and I had two nice career options from which to choose: a position as an assistant principal at a new middle school in Chicago (which I took) or a return to graduate school to study sociology (which I took a year later). I guess I was the last American to believe in the concept of progress.

"Come Saturday Morning" was not about me or a woman but about a relationship. The woman involved was a real woman, but I was real too. The song served to help define and normalize my entree to adulthood. The old, burning, narcissistic, and self-destructive question of "good" or "bad" girl was irrelevant and too silly to even consider. Polly was nei-ther. She was my friend, a woman's role unheard of back on the streets of south side Chicago: "Come Saturday Morning / I'm going away with my friend." We would do things together: "We'll Saturday spend / Till the end of the day." Things we would remember forever: "But we will re-member / Long after Saturday's gone."

The song helped others to see our private feelings of joy and to incor-porate them into the larger world of family. The mystery of life contin-ued, but it shifted its base of operation from women to community. Polly and I decided to have the soloist sing this song at our wedding. We wanted to partake in and continue the practice begun during the recent hippie countercultural era of having a personal if secular song performed at our wedding. Even then, we were a bit nervous when the Catholic priest in Weston, Missouri, cautioned us that, ahem, the song might be a bit inappropriate. Five years earlier, I might have used this song and the issue of appropriateness as weapons in the war against "The Establish-ment." But, now, I was real and the woman was real, so we calmly and maturely convinced the priest that this song was harmless to our faith, would not create scandal, and so on. And the medium for this "our song"? Well, there may be a copy of the Sandpipers' album in the stack of dusty old albums (rarely touched by human hands anymore) next to the stereo, but I am not sure. I do know that the sheet music we bought for the church organist and the soloist sits in the piano bench, to be occasion-ally pulled out and performed by our children when we hang around and play music on an otherwise slow day.

"Why": Annie Lennox

It's 1992, and it's been a long time between songs about women. As I assemble a family and a career, I find that my semantic and affective needs for music change. I share heavy metal with the young men in my life. I share classic rock with the old men in my life. I share Michael Jackson and Weird Al Yankovic with my children. Like all precocious parents, I share my children's music with my wife (i.e., flute, saxophone, clarinet, and piano performances of music composed by other old men whose names I cannot spell or pronounce). Usually, the concept "songs about women" emerges in a unit I teach in my "Sociology of Popular Music" class on the status of women in the popular music industry. But there, the talk is only about economics, politics, and ideologies. Somehow, I am usually able to sneak in a brief discussion of Suzy B. and Dion, but that discussion takes place in terms of the autobiographically depressing topic of the "early days" (good old days?) of rock 'n' roll.

Now, I find myself in a motel room in Tempe, Arizona. It's Saturday morning; the conference is over; and I'm getting ready to leave for home. The TV is on, as it always is, and MTV is providing a background context for my shower and shave, as it always does. As the haunting introduction to "Why" drifts out of the TV, I am drawn to it, to see what the video is all about. "Why" is an unusual song. It is an hypnotic ballad, and Annie Lennox sounds like a torch singer from even before my generation. She presents the image of the women who populate my world now, women who display contradiction and paradox, a melding of the old and the new, perhaps even a melding of the good and the bad. But in the postmodern world, it's all OK and it works. It works well.

The video begins with a view of Annie in front of a makeup mirror. I don't gaze at her directly, but I see her reflection in the mirror. I am witnessing Annie talking to herself. I immediately sense that Annie is disclosing a deep level of self to me because she is letting me see her without her makeup, while she is putting her makeup on. In the modern world, disclosure of self might have been signified by nudity, but that imagery lost its existential value long ago. (Is there a Hollywood star anymore who hasn't disclosed his or her body to audiences?) Annie is simultaneously beautiful and plain, feminist and feminine. She is serious about her feelings yet playful with herself and her self-adornment.

The lyrics tell the sad story of a relationship going bad, but the video gives no indication that Annie is vulnerable or crumbling under the weight of her loss. Instead, Annie tells us of her hurt and doubt while nonchalantly preparing herself for her powerful role as diva. In the end, Annie is honest with herself and her other (and me, the voyeur): "Don't think you know what I feel / You don't know what I feel."

Annie is a new kind of woman in the life of a middle-aged man like me. She is, like the postmodern period that spawned her, an accumulation of all the women (at least in my history) who preceded her. She is not merely a great rock singer, like Ann Wilson, or a sensuous chanteuse, like Stevie Nicks, or a seasoned tough-guy girl, like Bonnie Raitt, or a woman's woman, like k.d. lang, or a cutie, like Olivia Newton-John, or the woman you want to seduce you, like Grace Slick. She is all of them but, more precisely, can be any or all of them. Her self is like her face . . . ready to be transformed into anything she wants it to be.

I have many Annies in my life who flashed before my consciousness as I watched that video in my room: my daughter, who was nine going on nineteen, who can glide between basketball, Barbie dolls, *90210*, make-up, and daddy's lap; the young women at school, who can glide between hair styles, the environment, careers, feminism, and body scents. Annie Lennox helps me make sense of the post- (not extra-) marital women in my life by showing me how women, like life, are constantly changing. I'll bet even Dion likes Annie.

"I Knew I Loved You": Savage Garden

I first heard this very pretty pop song on FM radio in the car in 2001 while I was driving around the neighborhood doing errands—you know, typical weekend tasks, such as recycling and getting gas for the lawn mower. At first, I thought it was a new Smokey Bill Robinson song, given the high-pitched tenor voice of lead singer, Darren Hayes. It is such a pretty song, with a melody and harmony much like a butterfly navigating through a field of flowers. The story is of idealized love, romantic in ways not ordinarily attributed to middle-age men who are thought to prefer wallowing in harder rock experiences, such as the Rolling Stones and the Who. To wit, "I knew I loved you before I met you / I think I dreamed you into life." The story explains how this perfect woman will perfect a man: "A thousand angels dance around you / I am complete now that I've found you."

This is the kind of song that one cannot get out of one's head. It is really an excellent example of a pop song. The music industry, journalists, and fans all generally agree—or, more to the point, assume—what a pop song is all about. The assumption is based on the characteristics of the song per se: that a pop song is simple, banal, melodic, with inconsequential lyrics and interchangeable performers (e.g., Campbell 2009: 2–16). Sociologically, I prefer to conceptualize a pop song in terms of the experience of it in everyday life. Put differently, a pop song is itself a social construction, not an object. A pop song that works is one that makes you feel good, that you can hum anytime, that you can sing in the shower or when driving, that you never get tired of, that you get excited about when learning that it is next on the radio playlist, and that catches your full attention and is not just background noise. A pop song provides a pace for everyday life: as you drive to work, as you work on your computer, as you mow the lawn. Perhaps most important, you can picture yourself with someone special when the song is performed.

"I Knew I Loved You" fits the sociological definition of a pop song to a tee. I find myself humming the song, singing it in the shower, and never getting tired of hearing it on my CD player in the car—now that Savage Garden's hit is only played on 1990s oldies radio stations. Strangely enough, few people in my social universe really liked the song. My son Chris pretty much explained why. While he was home on break from the University of Miami, where he was studying jazz saxophone, we talked music as usual. He commented on my claim that it was a great song by saying, "Yah, if you are a twelve-year-old girl." He was right, and so was I. As I move up in age, I have come full circle in terms of some of the important features of popular music in my life. Savage Garden resurrected in me a key feature of the preadolescent pop music experience: naiveté. After sixty-odd years, I know better regarding the complexity of relationships. Staying married to the same woman for thirty-five-plus years is a project and adventure, not just a commitment. Savage Garden reminded me of the value of making space for simplicity in a relationship.

The video that accompanies "I Knew I Loved You" tells the story much better than I can. Darren Hayes sings his song while riding on a subway train. There is a very pretty girl sitting across from him who may or may not be real, but she is the object of his attention. When the lights suddenly go out in the train, we see Darren reaching out to touch her hand. Real or imagined? It makes no difference. All relationships are real. All romances are imagined. "I Knew I Loved You" is safely floating in the clouds where I can catch it for my iPhone or my iPad. When my daughter got married in New Orleans in 2010, I asked that the DJ play this song at her wedding reception. I danced to it with my wife.

And the Sixth Song Will Be . . .

The male experience of rock 'n' roll music is very complex and mysterious. I've always thought that women's experiences of rock 'n' roll were more observable affectively—is there a male equivalent of *Tiger Beat* or fan clubs? How men experience music culturally is a function of a number of interrelated factors. Biographical point is important because one's relationships with and perceptual stance toward women changes over time. In the present narrative, the women in view shifted position from Oedipalist pedestal of early adolescent infatuation to the security and comfort of daddy's lap.

Available cultural material both liberates and limits the process of sense making. In the present narrative, "Runaround Sue" provided plausible interpretations for both the ecstasy of infatuation (i.e., this must be a great girl because Dion sings a song about her) and the melancholia of breaking up (i.e., she doesn't love me because, as Dion warns me, she's really a bad girl). If "Runaround Sue" wasn't available to me, then the following lived experiences (among others) may have occurred: (1) another song may have created the same feelings in me for her; (2) another song may have led me to define her otherwise, say, as just another inaccessible girl; or (3) I would have loved her anyway and would have "found" a song to account for my feelings. In terms of research, this variability in the biographical use of culture could be examined more formally and systematically.

The prevailing historical and structural climates, and one's biographical perception of them, create the possibilities for certain aesthetic responses to music. In the present narrative, the end of hippie culture at the beginning of the 1970s (e.g., as illustrated by the sad finality of the Beatles' "The Long and Winding Road" in 1970, which was also played quite frequently on the juke box mentioned earlier), the drudgery of a personalized war that just wouldn't go away, the residuals of the hippie culture (e.g., the joint), and the prevailing Western inclination to operationalize historical themes in terms of the portraits that men paint of women all served to create the conditions for an introspective and ascetic lived experience like "Sweet Thing."

The importance of the situation in which rock music is experienced cannot be overstated. The situation elicits all these factors and melds them into lived experience. In the present narrative, the unbounded joy of hearing "Runaround Sue" while riding my bicycle on a Saturday evening was surely elicited and enhanced by the independence, speed, motion, and concentration provided by the uniquely adolescent experience of solitary bike riding in the big city.

The examination of rock 'n' roll music experiences as a feature of postmodern culture complements the current, widespread focus on film in cultural studies in several ways. First, rock 'n' roll music involves the use of a range of media. The media relaying rock 'n' roll changes rapidly, providing the researcher with the opportunity to examine the impact of changing media formats within the lifetime of particular audience members/respondents (cf. Altheide and Snow 1991). Second, rock music is experienced in an endless array of interactional situations, as opposed to the basic theater/home option involved in viewing film. Third, rock music increasingly incorporates a visual component that allows for comparison, as well as contrast, with film.

A clarification of the relative sampling merits of the case study presented here is in order. I would be a bit hard pressed to generalize too widely from my lived experiences of rock 'n' roll. Clearly, I have maintained a fairly romanticized style of dealing with women through rock 'n' roll. As indicated earlier, I do not ordinarily gravitate toward rock 'n' roll music that treats women harshly if not abusively. Thus, the present analysis underrepresents the sexist dimension of male rock 'n' roll that is clearly present and that feminist critics choose to highlight. Nevertheless, I believe that my example of "Runaround Sue" hints at the process of how cultural material that is potentially sexist enters the everyday life of men and is used to address situational problems with women in a sexist fashion. This type of early adolescent moralizing may not in itself be severe, but it could hypothetically initiate a pattern of sexist responses to situations invoking definitions and interpretations of women in later life.

Yet, the question remains: does rock 'n' roll music and culture support sexism in later life? The simple answer is, there is no simple answer. During the course of my interviews and conversations with male baby boomers, I rarely heard any indication that they sought or entertained negative meanings for women from rock 'n' roll. Aging men and women are more inclined to consolidate their feelings and normalize their relationships. Over the course of aging, any indication of sexism in the rock 'n' roll experience becomes increasingly subtle if at all present. Ideas about and feelings toward women have been long established. Using features of rock 'n' roll to pick fights or sustain conflict is simply too much work. Female baby boomers in my study generally feel the same way about men. Kat Fulton is a music therapist who works specifically with aging adults. In an interview with *Psychology Today* (Moore 2012), she notes that adults increasingly perceive and experience music as fun and a way to stay in contact with other people. We can infer that, with age, fun increasingly displaces advantage in importance.

FOUR

The Parental Self: Teaching Your Children Well

Popular music is endemic to modern family life, and this certainly applies to baby boomers. When they first married in the 1960s and 1970s, they constituted the first generation of Americans to introduce popular music into the formal wedding ceremony—beyond having Elvis sing "Hawaiian Honeymoon" at a wedding chapel in Las Vegas—sometimes with great effort. The "our songs" that couples insisted on playing in church, chapel, synagogue, or open field—in concert with the overall movement to personalize marriage ceremonies—ranged from Led Zeppelin's (romantic?) "Stairway to Heaven" to the Sandpipers' (truly romantic) "Come Saturday Morning" (Kotarba 1997).

As baby boomer newlyweds evolved into parents, popular music became a very important feature of self, perhaps more so than for any previous generation. Somebody's dad was cool, for example, if he had any semblance of good taste in rock 'n' roll music. Authenticity in music per se became relevant when it affected family leisure activities involving music.

The impact of rock 'n' roll on one's self as parent is possibly the most pervasive aspect of the rock 'n' roll experience in adulthood. Baby boomers grew up experiencing music as a major medium for communicating with parents—it provided both a semantic and a syntax for making sense together. Managing music illustrates one's skill at parenting, as well as one's style of parenting.

Standard scholarly and journalistic wisdom on rock 'n' roll argues that it has functioned largely to help establish adolescence as a distinctive stage in the life cycle while serving as a weapon in conflicts between adults and adolescents. The mass media have long contributed to this overstated, over-romanticized view of rock 'n' roll and adolescence. The rebellious imagery of Elvis Presley, for example, portrays a prevailing cultural myth that links rock 'n' roll with youthful rebellion, unbridled sexuality, cross-ethnic intimacy, and a wide range of delinquent activities (Garafolo 2008). The 1984 film *Footloose* portrays the plausible scenario in which fundamentally conservative, small-town adults view rock 'n' roll as an evil influence on their teenagers. Rock 'n' roll is portrayed in the film as the gauntlet that forces teenagers to choose between good and evil, either to obey their parents or to go dancing.

These cultural images support an ideological vision of youth culture that overemphasizes the independence and rebellion of teenagers. I argue that this history blurs the fact that there is and has always been much more diversity within youth culture (Kotarba 2002c). The kids on *American Bandstand* in the 1950s and early 1960s were all-American kids. They dressed modestly and neatly. They all chewed Beechnut gum, provided by the sponsor of the program. Above all, they were extremely well behaved. The boys and girls, especially the "regulars," tended to match up as boyfriends and girlfriends, not as potentially promiscuous dates and mates. *American Bandstand* probably represented most teenagers in American society at that time. And teenagers could not participate in activities like *American Bandstand* without the approval, if not support, of their parents. After all, someone had to drive the kids to the studio or at least give them permission and money to take the bus there, just as someone had to provide the television and permit watching *American Bandstand* at home.

Baby boomers appear to have been more likely to be cautious supporters of their children's—and grandchildren's—rock 'n' roll activities than outright critics. This somewhat passive, if not permissive, style of parenting is not new to baby boomers; in fact, they learned it from their parents. For every Elvis Presley fan in the 1950s and 1960s whose parents threatened disowning, there was an *American Bandstand* fan whose parent (mom?) was likely to sit next to her in front of the TV and watch Fabian and Frankie Avalon make all the girls sigh (Stuessy and Lipscomb 1999).

There is a greater tendency among parents—apparently across ethnic groups and social classes—to manage rock 'n' roll as though their teenagers are children who need to be nurtured and protected, rather than as adolescents who must be controlled, sanctioned, and feared. At a Metallica concert in Houston several years ago, for example, numerous teenagers indicated that their parents did not approve of heavy metal music for various reasons (e.g., volume, distortion, immorality, and potential affiliation with evil entities like Satanism). Yet these same parents carpooled their teenagers and friends to the Astrodome on an afternoon that was a school day and, in most cases, bought or provided the money for tickets. A similar situation exists among African American and Latino parents as well as Anglo parents in terms of the popularity of rap music among their teenagers (Kotarba 1994a). Mass media–generated images of obstinate, if not rebellious, youth generally ignore the reflexive relationship between teenagers and their parents. As long as teenagers live at home as legal, financial, and moral dependents—that is, as children—their parents provide the resources for creating rock 'n' roll identities (e.g., allowances, free time, and fashionable hip-hop clothing). Some parents then respond negatively to the identities they helped create by controlling, criticizing, sanctioning, and punishing their teenagers for living out their rock 'n' roll–inspired identities—responding to them as if they were autonomous, responsible adults.

THE GOOD FIT BETWEEN ROCK 'N' ROLL MUSIC AND THE FAMILY

Lay and professional critics have long cast a wary eye on children's pop culture. They have been especially critical of materials emanating from the electronic media. These materials include television violence (which allegedly leads to violent behavior among young viewers), music videos (some of which contain sexist messages), and rap music (which is criticized for many reasons; cf. Wilson 1989). Rock 'n' roll music has been critiqued most often and most harshly, being designated as a "social problem" ever since its inception over sixty years ago. After a brief review of the criticism of the moral and psychological merits of popular music, I add some balance to the debate by presenting an inventory of some of the positive features of rock 'n' roll music (Kotarba 1994a).

The case against rock 'n' roll began in the 1950s with dramatic efforts to eliminate rock 'n' roll (Martin and Seagrave 1988). Organized burnings of Elvis Presley records, because of their alleged association with sinfulness and sexuality, were common in fundamentalist communities. In the 1960s, critics argued that rock 'n' roll music was unpatriotic, communistic, and the cause of drug abuse. In the 1970s and 1980s, the criticism became organized and sophisticated. Middle-class activist organizations, such as the Parents Music Resource Center led by Tipper Gore, opposed rock 'n' roll for its alleged deleterious effects on the health of young people. In the 1990s, we find several court cases in which the prosecution and the defense attempted to legally link rock 'n' roll with suicide and criminal behavior, respectively (Hill 1992).

Allan Bloom (1987), a professor of social thought at the University of Chicago, argued that American universities are in a state of crisis because of their lack of commitment to traditional intellectual standards. Bloom further argued that young people live in a state of intellectual poverty: "Those students do not have books, they most emphatically do have music" (68). Plato, Socrates, and Aristotle all viewed music as a natural mechanism for expressing the passions and preparing the soul for reason. University students' overwhelming choice in music today, rock music,

has one appeal only, a barbaric appeal, to sexual desire—not love, not
eros, but sexual desire undeveloped and untutored. . . . Young people
know that rock has the beat of sexual intercourse. . . . Rock music
provides premature ecstasy and is like the drug with which it is al-
lied. . . . But, as long as they have the Walkman on, they cannot hear
what the great tradition has to say. And, after its prolonged use, when
they take it off, they find they are deaf. (68–81)

Critics, whether in the academy or in the mass media, have generally
viewed rock 'n' roll as either a social problem or a major cause of other
social problems. In the contrary, I believe that the effects of rock 'n' roll
music on its audiences vary considerably. In many different ways, rock
'n' roll integrates families and serves as a bridge across generations. This
generational bridge allows children, adolescents, and adults to share
communication, affect, morality, ethics, and meanings.

Critics focus on the dysfunctions of rock 'n' roll because they ignore
the increasingly obvious fact that rock 'n' roll, broadly defined, is pervasive in American culture. We now have four generations of Americans
who have grown up with rock 'n' roll music. For them, rock 'n' roll music
is the preeminent form of popular music. It serves as the soundtrack for
everyday life, providing the context for phenomena such as commercials,
patriotic events, high school graduations, political conventions. The functional or positive experiences of rock music simply do not attract the
attention of observers such as journalists and social scientists, whose
work is structured around the concept of "the problem." To understand
the pervasiveness of rock 'n' roll and its positive as well as negative
functions, I have reconceptualized it as a feature of children's culture
shared by the entire family.[4]

ROCK 'N' ROLL AS A FEATURE OF CHILDREN'S CULTURE

Conventional social scientific thinking posits rock 'n' roll as a key element of youth culture. The concept "youth culture," which can be traced
at least as far back as the works of Talcott Parsons (1951), is commonly
used to denote those everyday practices conducted by adolescents, which
serve (1) to identify them as a specific generational cohort separate from
children and adults, (2) as common apparatus for the clarification and
resolution of conflict with adults, and (3) to facilitate the process of socialization or transformation into adulthood.

Conventional thinking isolates certain socioeconomic-cultural developments since World War II to construct an explanation for the historically integrated coevolution of teenagers and rock 'n' roll (Frith 1981). This
theory argues that teenagers were a product of the postwar family. The
general cultural portrait of this family is one of middle-class aspiration (if
not achievement), suburban orientation, affluence, and consumption.

Teenagers in the 1950s composed not only a demographic bulge in the American population but also an economic force. Teenagers are viewed as a product of the following formula: allowances + leisure time + energy + parental indulgence. Rock 'n' roll music became an available and useful commodity to sell to teenagers. The music could be readily duplicated; the themes could directly address the angst and adventure of adolescence; and the 45 record could be designed to be disposable through the process of the top 40.

As the postwar generation grew into adulthood in the 1960s, they took the previously fun-filled rock 'n' roll and turned it into a medium for political dissent and moral/cultural opposition to the generation of their parents. Critics have argued, however, that as the baby boomers reached full adulthood, many traded in their political passion for rock 'n' roll for rock 'n' roll–oriented country music (e.g., Alabama and Brooks and Dunn) and light rock, pop, jazz, and so on. Succeeding generations of teenagers consume the hegemonic cultural pabulum of formulaic rock 'n' roll and MTV (Grossberg 1992a).

As I have argued, a powerful cultural experience such as growing up with rock 'n' roll cannot be simply left behind by movement through the life cycle. One would reasonably expect to find at least some residual effects of rock 'n' roll on adult baby boomers. If rock 'n' roll affected the way they dated, mated, and resisted, then one would reasonably expect rock 'n' roll music to affect the way they work, parent, construct and service relationships, and in other ways accomplish adulthood. Paradoxically, the presence of rock 'n' roll in the lives of adults as well as adolescents can be discovered by locating it in the lives and culture of children (Kotarba 2002c).

Postmodern social thought reminds us that contemporary social life is mass mediated. Culture is less a reflection of some underlying, formal, firm, structural reality than it is an entity in its own right (Baudrillard 1979). Postmodernism allows the observer to see things not previously visible. For example, postmodernism recently has let us see gender as a critical factor in the process of writing history. Instead of gazing directly at the alleged facts of the past, postmodernism allows historians to focus on the process by which history itself is written different ways by different authors. Similarly, postmodernism lets the sociologist analyze cultural forms like rock 'n' roll as free-floating texts with their own styles of production, disseminations, interpretations, and applications to everyday life situations. Therefore, at least hypothetically, rock 'n' roll is no longer (if it ever was) simply a reflection of the structural positions of adolescents in Western societies, no longer a possession of youth. Rather, cultural items in the postmodern world become available to anyone in society for their individual and subcultural interpretation, modification, and application. To see rock 'n' roll as a feature of children's culture helps us see its presence in all generations. The concept "children's culture" denotes those everyday practices that are (1) used by children to interpret and master everyday life; (2) created, acquired, disseminated, and used by adults to construct and define parental relationships with children; and (3) ordinarily associated with children and childhood yet are used by adolescents and adults to interpret, master, or enjoy certain everyday life situations. Children experience rock 'n' roll as children. Adolescents experience rock 'n' roll to extend childhood. Adults experience rock 'n' roll to relive childhood.

Adolescents as Children

As mentioned earlier, standard wisdom rock 'n' roll argues that it has functioned largely to establish adolescence as a distinct stage in the life cycle. Furthermore, rock 'n' roll is seen as a weapon in conflicts between adults and adolescents. This standard wisdom clearly misunderstood the actual nature and meaning of adolescence in post–World War II and beyond. The argument that adolescence is a distinctive stage between childhood and adulthood is oversimplified. Adolescence is marked by both childhood and adult orientations. Teenagers in American society may have aspired to the privileges and responsibilities of adulthood (e.g., behavioral independence, access to work and careers, less-restricted sex, residential mobility, and absence of parental supervision and management). The truth has been that teenagers have continued to relish the pleasures of childhood, although having occasional difficulty integrating them into an emerging adulthood. These pleasures include lack of responsibility for one's decisions, embodied but nonsexual pleasures, fantasy, nongendered identities, and memberships (e.g., tomboy persona). These pleasures are present in both the semantics and syntax of the rock 'n' roll idiom, as will be illustrated below. The experience and enjoyment of these pleasures in adolescence have largely escaped the purview of professional, critical, and lay observers of adolescence. Our culture has been more readily willing to refer to them in terms of immaturity, annoyance, risk-taking, irresponsibility, and laziness.

These cultural images support an ideological vision of youth culture that overemphasizes the independence, rebellion, and cohesiveness among teenagers. A revisionist or postmodernist reading of this history finds much more diversity within youth culture. For every Elvis Presley fan in the 1950s and 1960s, there was an *American Bandstand* fan. *American Bandstand*—especially in its early days, when it was broadcast live after school from Philadelphia—portrayed rock 'n' roll in ways much milder and more acceptable to adults as well as teenagers. The kids on *American Bandstand* were all-American kids. They dressed modestly and neatly. They all chewed Beechnut gum, provided by the sponsor of the program. Above all, they were extremely well behaved. The boys and girls, especially the "regulars," tended to match up as boyfriends and girlfriends, not as potentially promiscuous dates and mates. *American Bandstand* probably represented most teenagers in American society at that time. And, teenagers could not participate in activities like *American Bandstand* without the approval, if not support, of their parents. After all, someone had to drive the kids to the studio or at least give them permission and money to take the bus there, just as someone had to provide the television and permit watching *American Bandstand* at home.

From the teenagers' perspective, rock 'n' roll is commonly an extension of childhood experiences. The Summer of Love in 1967 is the case in point. Mass media accounts treat the Monterey Music Festival and Haight-Ashbury as benchmarks in the emergence of the youth counter culture. The Summer of Love marked the fulfillment of rock 'n' roll as an instrument of adolescent rebellion, within a context of heavy drug use, free love, and political liberation—a clash between young people's values and those of their parents. The media argued that the political events of the late 1960s institutionalized and radicalized the unbridled, individualistic, and existentially youthful rebellion of the 1950s and early 1960s.

A postmodernist reexamination of these events suggests that the innocence of middle-class, postwar, baby-boom childhood served as the primary metaphor for these young people. High status was attributed to the "flower child," whom the counterculture posited as the innocent who simply rejected the oppression of the adult establishment. Women in the movement with high status were known as "earth mothers," who nurtured themselves and their peers through natural foods, folk arts, and the ability to roll good joints for the group. Whereas the mass media stresses the centrality of Jimi Hendrix and Jim Morrison to the music of this period, more child-like songs like Peter, Paul, and Mary's "Puff, the Magic Dragon" and Jefferson Airplane's "White Rabbit" (inspired by Alice in Wonderland) were at least as significant. The 1960s generation popularized the use of animation as a format for rock 'n' roll (e.g., the Beatles' *Yellow Submarine*). Perhaps most interesting to my argument is the way the 1960s generation drifted away from the adult world of commercialized and confined concert halls to the park-like atmosphere of the open air concert festival, where the audience could play with Frisbees, beach balls, and other toys.

Adolescents have since continued to experience rock 'n' roll qua children at play. In 1984, Van Halen's "Jump" was a very popular pop song. Many lay and professional critics of hard rock chose to interpret the song as an invitation to youthful suicide. It appeared that the kids did not. At the Van Halen concert held in the Summit in Houston that year, the fans—who appeared to range mostly from fourteen to seventeen years of age—let out a collective scream when Eddie Van Halen began the song with the now famous keyboard riff. At the chorus, when David Lee Roth shouted "jump," 18,000 teenagers did just that: they all jumped up together like a bunch of little kids in the playground during recess. I witnessed the same exuberance during a concert in Houston during Van Halen's 2007 reunion tour—when they brought back original front man David Lee Roth, the Clown Prince of Power Pop. Given the aging of the audience for Van Halen, however, the jump was on average not quite as high as it was before.

Rave parties that were first seen in the United States in the 1990s are often designed to appear like children's playgrounds or carnivals. Fun was the key feature sought. Bounce castles, inflatable trampoline-like houses are common, as are ring and bean bag toss games. Glow sticks, necklaces, and bracelets are sold and played with as toys. Many of the very creative invitation cards designed for rave parties look much like children's birthday party invitations (Kotarba 1994c).

Even the darker moments of rock 'n' roll have their child-like attributes. Teenage fans commonly experience heavy metal music as a mechanism for managing lingering, childhood anxieties. Metallica's "Enter Sandman" was a popular video on MTV during 1991 and 1992. As part of an ethnographic study of homeless teenagers, we asked these kids to talk about their tastes in music and musical activities. This particular video was very popular with them. We asked them specifically to interpret a very old, scary looking man in the video. This was the sandman, sitting in a rocking chair in the corner of the thirteen-year-old boy's bedroom. The street kids tended to see the man as a reflection of their own real nightmare experiences, such as physically abusive parents and sexually abusive adults in drug-infested neighborhoods. In a contrasting set of interviews with upper middle-class kids, we commonly heard them say that the man represented nightmares, but only the inconsequential fantasy nightmares involving mythical figures like the bogeyman. This study clearly established a social class distinction in the interpretation of rock 'n' roll music. Interestingly, we found very little difference in taste of rock 'n' roll by social class membership. Rock 'n' roll is simply that universal in our society and among youth in general. Homeless and privileged kids like the same music; it is just that rich kids have dads who buy them the best tickets to all the hot concerts (Kotarba 1994b). And, all kids like rap!

Children as Children

The pervasive mass media increasingly expose young children to rock 'n' roll. The Teenage Mutant Ninja Turtle rock concert tour, Saturday morning television (e.g., the M.C. Hammer cartoon program), digital performers like the Gorillaz, and interactive media such as Nintendo's Guitar Hero all focus on pre-adolescent audiences.

Beyond simple marketing, rock 'n' roll informs our general cultural views of children. *Honey, I Blew Up the Kid* was a popular comedy in 1992. The story line had a bumbling, (baby boomer) scientist father mistakenly turning his infant into a colossus. As the child innocently marched down a boulevard in Las Vegas, he grabbed the large, neon-lit guitar from the Hard Rock Café signpost and proceeded to pretend to play a rock 'n' roll song. (A generic, rock-a-billy song was actually playing in the film's background.) The guitar served as a toy for the baby. The imagery suggested the baby as adolescent, an absurdity that helped establish the overall absurdity of the story.

Young children can grasp rock 'n' roll even when it is not intentionally produced for or marketed to them. When Los Lobos covered the 1950s hit "La Bamba," in the 1990s, it became a favorite among elementary school-age children. Like many rock 'n' roll songs, young kids find its simple lyrics silly and its dance beat fun. As country music broadens its appeal by "crossing over" to rock and pop music audiences, it also creates an audience of children. Billy Ray Cyrus's rockabilly hit "Achy Breaky Heart" became a fun song for many children in the early 1990s. More recently, Trains' "Hey Soul Sister," has achieved the same status in 2011.

Rock 'n' roll music has now become a staple in the elementary school classroom. A very popular instructional system called "Schoolhouse Rock!" enables the teacher to teach grammar, multiplications, history, and science to a rock 'n' roll soundtrack. "Schoolhouse Rock!" is a series of fifty-two educational short films featuring songs about regular curriculum topics. The shorts were broadcast on the ABC television network between 1973 and 1986. They were then broadcast infrequently during the 1990s and 2000s, with additional shows created between 1993 and 1996. An additional short, "I'm Gonna Send Your Vote to College," was created for the 30th anniversary video release in 2003. Patricia is a third-grade public school teacher who uses "Schoolhouse Rock!" videos frequently. The pervasiveness of rock 'n' roll in children's culture is exemplified by Patricia's—a middle-age elementary school teacher—statement that it does not make great sense to try to classify "Schoolhouse Rock!" as rock, jazz or pop: "My kids just know it as music. The songs all sound very familiar, energetic, fun."

Adults as Children

Adults who grew up on rock 'n' roll may want to relive the fun, excitement and innocence of their earlier music experiences. This can happen two ways. First, adults may simply retrieve the past through nostalgia. In many cities, oldies or classic rock music stations are the most popular radio stations, catering to an audience approximately twenty-four to forty-five years of age and up. Rock 'n' roll nostalgia also appears in the guise of circa 1950s and 1960s clubs. These clubs are often decorated in postwar diner motif, offering period food such as meat loaf sandwiches and malted milk shakes. Parents and their children dine to piped-in oldies, within an atmosphere resembling that of the *Happy Days* sit-com.

Rock 'n' roll nostalgia is interesting because of the types of music chosen by programmers to attract and please their audiences. The music is typically 1950s style rockabilly or early 1960s pop rock (e.g., the Beach Boys and Motown groups). The primary audience for oldies programming, however, grew up with the somewhat harsher and harder music of the later 1960s (e.g., psychedelia and antiwar music). Most baby boomers will forsake their own music for the easygoing, apolitical fun music of their older siblings. In the language of postmodernism, the oldies culture is a simulacrum (cf. Baudrillard 1983). It never existed in its original state as it is now presented to consumers. Again, adults commonly choose to relive the child-like side of their reconstructed adolescence, not the adult side.

Second, adults may engage in continuous rock 'n' roll experiences that are constructed in the present. Many adults, especially males, maintain their original interest in rock 'n' roll. They are visible at live concerts of 1960s, 1970s, and 1980s performers who are still "on the road" (e.g., the Beach Boys, Rolling Stones, the Red Hot Chili Peppers, Van Halen, Metallica, Aerosmith, Crosby, Stills and Nash, and Black Sabbath). They continue to buy recorded music, but much less than teenagers do. An intriguing bonding and gift-giving ritual among middle-class and middle-age adult males is the exchange of tape dubs. One fan will purchase a new recording (preferably on compact disc) and proceed to dub high quality cassette tape copies for distribution to neighbors, coworkers, business associates, and others with similar tastes. Van Morrison fans are a good example. These are all fun activities.

The baby boomer generation's attempts to maintain the feeling of childhood through rock 'n' roll extends into its encounter with adulthood. Through the 1980s and 1990s, the baby boomer generation has been the strongest supporter of contemporary versions of the rock 'n' roll festival. Every large and most medium-size cities now have what are referred to as "shed venues." These outdoor concert sites, such as Ravinia in Chicago, Wolf Trap in Washington DC, Zilker Park in Austin and the Mitchell Pavilion in Houston, serve as the setting for baby boomers to bring their blankets and their picnic baskets—and often their children—to hear concerts by New Age performers. New Age music, by the way, fits my broad definition of rock 'n' roll. It is simply mellow, electronically amplified music appreciated by adults who want to extend their rock 'n' roll experiences, but who for physical or status/cultural reasons choose to give up the volume and anxiety of pure rock 'n' roll.

Adults may also use rock 'n' roll as a medium for rebellion. Practical and proven strategies developed during adolescence to enrage parents and other adults are retrieved to use against current opponents, such as wives. I have heard of men who turn up their stereos at home simply to aggravate their wives. In contrast, I have also heard of wives who banish their husbands to the basement or the garage to play their loud music, similar to the shaming banishment of a cigarette-smoking spouse to the backyard. Are these examples of "childish" behaviors?

Adults as Parents

As we have seen, members of all generations use rock 'n' roll music in everyday life. The major argument of this discussion, however, is that rock 'n' roll also serves as a bridge across the generations. Children, adolescents, and adults share rock 'n' roll. As one would easily guess, much of this sharing takes place within the family. Yet, contrary to common wisdom, we will argue that much of this sharing is functional and positive: rock 'n' roll helps integrate families.

From the early days of Elvis Presley to current issues surrounding rap music, our mass culture has portrayed rock 'n' roll as a source of tension within families (Martin and Segrave 1988). Whether this conflict is over lyrics or volume or whatever, the fact is that children could not experience rock 'n' roll without the implicit if not explicit support of their parents (as we have seen in the case of *American Bandstand* and Metallica). The cultural pervasiveness of rock 'n' roll lets rock 'n' roll function in many different ways in the family, much like religion or television have. I will now present an inventory of these—largely taken-for-granted—positive features of rock 'n' roll.

Mother and Daughter Bonding

Rock 'n' roll has always served as a special commonality between mothers and daughters. They shared Elvis Presley in the 1950s, Frankie Avalon and the Beatles in the 1960s, and Neil Diamond in the 1970s. In the feminist era of the 1980s and 1990s, however, the object of sharing shifted to other women. Madonna is the case in point.

Madonna represents a rock 'n' roll phenomenon that is attractive to both mothers and daughters. Madonna is a multifaceted star whose appeal rests on lifestyle, clothing style, and attitude as well as musical performance. During the Houston stop on the "Like a Virgin" tour, I interviewed a number of mother-daughter pairs who attended. The pairs typically were dressed alike, in outfits such as black bustier and short black skirts, with matching jewelry. During the interviews, they talked about Madonna in similar ways and appeared more like friends than family. In virtually all cases, they noted a distinct lack of true appreciation of Madonna by the men in their lives (e.g., fathers, husbands, brothers, and boyfriends who may look at Madonna and only see a sex object). In most cases, the mothers indicated that Madonna served to bring them closer to their daughters. Other female rock 'n' roll performers who fit this catego-ry today include Carrie Underwood, Katy Perry, and Beyonce.

Father and Son Bonding

Fathers and sons also use rock 'n' roll music to bond, but in different ways than one might expect. Fathers who learned to play guitar in the 1960s and 1970s teach their sons how to play. Sharing music is difficult, since the younger generation today continues the traditional ideological belief that their music is better than that of their parents. Fathers and sons are considerably more vehement than women in their allegiance to their generation's music. During my research on the rave phenomenon in Houston (Kotarba 1994c, 2007), I heard one sixteen-year-old boy exclaim: "I hate my dad's music. He listens to that old shit, like Led Zeppelin." On the other hand, recent trends like rave (i.e., dance parties held in clandes-tine locations, to the beat of loud synthesized music) display a renais-sance in the 1960s counterculture. Psychedelia is "in," for example, with LSD as the drug of choice and lighting provided by mood lamps. Teenag-ers see rave as a way of retrieving the romance and simplicity of the 1960s. In effect, these kids accept their parents' claim that growing up in the 1960s was special. Another example is Deadhead fathers and their sons sharing the Grateful Dead experience—as well as their Deadhead T-shirts.

I am also a bit surprised to see the extent to which fathers share Guitar Hero, and the more recent Guitar Band franchise, with their sons. These are plastic guitar and music video games introduced back in 2005. One plays along on a pretend guitar with music and video on a computer or TV screen. These games were among the top Christmas presents over the past few years, but have waned in popularity recently. There are now different versions of Guitar Hero available, including Van Halen, Aero-smith, and Metallica. Guitar Hero has been one toy dad and son could fight over beneath the Christmas tree. Bob is a sixty-one-year-old grocery store manager who purchased Guitar Hero for his then nineteen-year-old college sophomore son for Christmas. Although Bob never learned to play the guitar, he can share the guitar experience with his garage band, lead guitar player son:

> It's a lot of fun. We played guitar hero all day Christmas day. I would never play air guitar at home with my kids—they would think I'm nuts. You should have seen my wife on Christmas—she thinks I'm nuts.

In my own family, I recall a very special rock 'n' roll experience with my oldest son, when he was five years old. We were driving out to a fishing hole in my old pickup truck, when the local hard rock radio station began playing songs from the Van Halen album 1984. This is one of my all-time favorite albums and, in a sociological sense, definitive of the state of rock music in the mid-1980s. When the pounding, driving anthem "Panama" came on the radio, it began with the loud rumble of a motorcycle taking off. Chris proceeded to jump around in his seat to the excitement of what he knew as the "motorcycle song." Like any proud baby boomer father, a tear left my eye when I realized that my son was OK . . . he liked rock 'n' roll.

Family Leisure Activities

Rock 'n' roll fits well with the burgeoning family leisure and vacation industry. Family theme parks typically have some attraction related to rock 'n' roll, such as the complete mock-up of a 1950s small town main street in the Fiesta Texas Theme Park in San Antonio. The artists performing at the amphitheaters in the Six Flags parks have included oldies/reunion bands such as REO Speedwagon, an Eagles reunion band, Chicago, and the latest version of the Jefferson Airplane/Starship.

Whereas the concept "family entertainment" in the 1950s, 1960s, and 1970s referred to phenomena such as wholesome television programming, Walt Disney films and home games, it increasingly refers to rock 'n' roll today. The rock 'n' roll presented usually addresses a common denominator acceptable to both parents and children, especially rockabilly.

Take the modern family vacation. Baby boomers made the notion of a family vacation to a theme park popular and indeed commonplace in the burgeoning family leisure and vacation industry.

The issue of authenticity is relevant to this type of family entertainment. While conducting interviews at the Fiesta Texas Theme Park in San Antonio, I spoke with James, a fifty-eight-year-old insurance executive who has taken his family of five to numerous theme parks, ranging from Disneyland in California to Disneyworld in Florida. I asked James to unpack his understanding of musical authenticity, and learned that for him determining whether the rock-a-billy, family-oriented musical performance that is pervasive at theme parks is authentic or not was a complex and nuanced undertaking. On the one hand, it is not authentic; the actors and dancers are not performing authentic rock-a-billy music—in terms of arrangements, instrumentation, and lyrics—as Elvis or Buddy Holly did. On the other hand, the music is authentic insofar as it fits the category of rock-a-billy better than any other available category of music, as intended by the producers and show directors. Still, it is inauthentic to the degree that its original fans—or current sophisticated fans like James—probably do not accept it as "real" rock-a-billy. Nevertheless, for James the theme park music is moderately—but acceptably—inauthentic (or perhaps sufficiently authentic, if you will).

Inauthenticity—for James and others—is not necessarily a bad thing that eliminates certain musical performances from radio or concert consideration. Having the perceived ability to differentiate authenticity from inauthenticity can index a valued self. As James concluded:

> I love it. Going to see one of those bullshit shows is great. I get to be the music expert in my family, for a change. I can poke fun at them, but the kids are OK with that. They figure dad's an old guy—he should know.

This is a clear example of how the mastery of authenticity work—regardless of the outcome of this work—contributes to a valued self. Indeed, this skill may be more valuable interactionally and internally than the actual mastery of the content of music (e.g., song titles, artists' names, lyrics, styles, date of popularity, level of popularity).

Religious Socialization

An integral segment of the self-as-parent is moral if not religious or spiritual socialization. Rock 'n' roll functions as a mechanism for teaching religious beliefs and values in many families, whether or not rock 'n' roll is compatible with the particular family's religious orientation. For mainstream Protestant denominations, rock 'n' roll increasingly fits with faith.

For example, when Amy Grant played in Houston several years ago, her music was loud and fast (e.g., seven piece band with double drummers and double lead guitars). Parents accompanying their children to the concert peppered the audience. One young father, in his forties, brought his wife and ten year-old daughter to the concert, which he learned about at his Lutheran church. When I asked him about the compatibility of Christian rock music with Christianity, he stated:

> We love Amy Grant. She is married and tours with her husband, which is not the case with regular rock stars. Her songs are full of Christian messages. Any way you can get the message of Christ to your kids is OK with us.

The variety of Christian rock 'n' roll styles is growing. A particularly intriguing version is Christian heavy metal (Kotarba 1991). One rock club in Houston routinely books Christian heavy metal bands on Sunday evenings. One evening, they booked a Christian speed metal band, White Cross, which played extremely loud and fast music about Christ. I talked to several parents, with ages ranging from the thirties to the fifties, who accompanied their children to the concert. The parents were very polite, clean cut, middle-class, Southern Baptists surrounded by a sea of punk rockers and headbangers. They struck me as being much like the parents of the *American Bandstand* generation discussed above. They created the opportunity for their teenagers to attend the concert by carpooling them and their friends in from the suburbs. They hoped that the message emanating from the long-haired rockers was indeed Christian, but they wanted to see for themselves that Satan was not infiltrating the event.

Certain fundamentalist Christian denominations tend to view rock 'n' roll of any kind as evil, whether under the guise of Christian rock or not. Parents in this faith focus their attention on rock 'n' roll as a way of establishing moral boundaries for their children. For example, a very popular video among fundamentalist youth ministers is titled *Rock 'n' Roll: A Search for God*. The producer, Eric Holmberg, displays numerous rock album covers to illustrate his argument that rockers, especially heavy metal rockers, advertently or inadvertently proclaim satanic messages. Mr. Holmberg discusses the ways some rock groups, like AC/DC, are explicitly satanic (e.g., "Hell's Bells"), whereas others may be inadvertent tools of Satan (e.g., "Cheap Trick"). He argues that some groups, like Queen and Led Zeppelin, perform songs that contain satanic messages that can only be understood when the songs are played backwards; this phenomenon is known as "backmasking."

For fundamentalist parents, rock 'n' roll functions as a convenient and accessible way of teaching their children clearly and directly that Satan and evil are present in today's world and can take various attractive forms. Ironically, Christian rock and satanic rock dramatically illustrate the ongoing battle between good and evil for many Christians. An example comes from an ethnographic study I conducted on an all-ages rock music club (Kotarba and Wells 1987). This live-music club hosted three different styles of heavy metal music in the same weekend. There were speed metal bands on Friday evenings, satanic metal bands on Saturday evenings, and Christian heavy metal bands on Sunday evenings. When it became apparent that many of the same teenagers attended both the satanic and Christian concerts, my colleague and I asked several teens about this. Bobby, a sixteen-year-old Latino fan who saw the two concerts as a competition, said:

> Oh, yes, Helstar (a popular satanic metal band in Houston, Texas) is bad. They always bad-mouth the priests and even the Bishop. The music is heavy, man, like a real battle, like good angels against bad angels. Who's gonna win? Oh, I think the bad dudes will win; they're meaner.

I have never been really sure just how seriously metal fans take the satanic, spiritual, and combative portrayals imbedded into heavy metal shtick. I mean, I assume everyone has seen the Gene Simmons (of KISS) suburban family reality TV program, *Family Jewels*—I watched it once for about three minutes before switching over to a *Seinfeld* rerun. Gene is not going to hell—he is going to the bank. In any event the type of analysis Bobby gave was common among heavy metal fans raised Catholic and Southern Baptists. I think the kids' religious training taught them less about the theology underlying the conflict between good and evil, than the drama and excitement permeating the atmosphere of the battle.

Oh, and by the way, parents typically drove their underage children to the all-ages club. Also typically, many young club-goers insisted their parents drop them off about a block away at a Denny's Restaurant so their friends would not see that their parents had to drive them.

Moral Socialization

Rock 'n' roll functions as a mechanism for articulating general moral rules and values for particular groups. Although the Parents Music Resource Center had been broadly based politically, it supported the religious right's concern for the threat rock 'n' roll poses to the moral, physical, and psychological health of their children (Weinstein 1991). For middle-class and upwardly mobile African American parents, rap music clarifies the issue of gender abuse within their community (Light 1992). In a more institutionalized sense, rap music is becoming the medium of choice among inner-city teachers for transmitting emerging moral messages. For example, rap music is now allowed in the Houston public schools for student talent shows. The local news regularly highlights school programs in which students use the rap idiom to convey antismoking and antidrug messages.

Historical Socialization

Families use rock 'n' roll to relay a sense of history to their children. For example, every year on Memorial Day in Houston, various veterans' organizations sponsor a concert and rally at the Miller Outdoor Theater. Most of the veterans present fought in Vietnam, the first war for which rock 'n' roll served as the musical soundtrack. Increasingly, however, the veterans present fought in the wars in Iraq and Afghanistan. Many veterans bring their children to the event. Among all the messages and information available to the kids is the type of music popular during the war. A popular band regularly invited to perform is the Guess Who, whose "American Woman" was a major anthem among soldiers in Vietnam. I have observed fathers explaining the song to their children and grandchildren, who would otherwise view it as just another of dad or grandpa's old songs. In interview, the fathers explained that the song had different meanings for different men. For some, it reminded them of girlfriends back home who broke up with them during the war. For others, the title was enough to remind them of their faithful girlfriends back home. For still others, the song reminded them of the occasions when they were sitting around camp, smoking pot and listening to any American rock 'n' roll songs available as a way of bridging the many miles between them and home. In Houston, Juneteenth and Cinco de

Mayo activities function much the same way for African American and Latino families, respectively, invoking hip hop and Tejano music.

I have only touched on the many ways rock 'n' roll music functions positively for people, especially in terms of family integration. The illustrations certainly do not represent all rock 'n' roll experiences in a systematically sampled way. My generalizations are based largely on the experiences and perceptions of white, middle-class rock 'n' roll fans and their families. Nevertheless, I would argue that the principles of culture use discussed here apply across subpopulations in our society, as we will see below.

OUR PARENTS' MUSIC

In 2002, I embarked on a study of the everyday life impact of rock 'n' roll music on family relations (Kotarba 2003). In my previous research on popular music, I often talked to parents about their children and rock 'n' roll, and I talked to children about their parents and rock 'n' roll. As symbolic interactionists (Blumer 1969) and ethnomethodologists (Mehan and Wood 1975) remind us, social realities are created and negotiated in actual everyday life situations. I wanted to create situations that resembled naturally occurring situations in which conversations about rock 'n' roll would appear typical. I arranged a series of videotaped interviews, in which I encouraged a parent to talk about rock 'n' roll with his or her child. The goal is to show how critical popular music is to family culture, and to celebrate the many ways parents and children use popular music to express their feelings and construct their self-identities. The conversations were informal, and largely conducted at respondents' homes.[5]

I drew participants in my project from various communities and ethnic groups in Houston. I located them through personal contacts, class announcements at the University of Houston, Houston Community College, and personal networking.

Participants in my project represent the following ethnic groups: Polish American, Chinese American, African American, Mexican American, and Anglo American. Parental occupations include: unemployed, office administrator, sales clerk, teacher, real estate broker, electrical technician, and so on. The intergenerational styles of music explored include—among others—hard rock and punk rock; rhythm and blues and rap; traditional gospel and pop gospel; alternative rock and classical music; and Tejano music and rock en Espanol.

Participants in the project had a great time talking about music and family life. Although all of the participants noted that popular music fairly regularly enters normal family interaction, they were generally surprised to learn explicitly of each other's values, desires, and expectations of the popular music experience. Topics that came up during our conver-

sations include gift-giving, discipline, religious socialization, political socialization, entertainment, bonding, escape, and work. I will discuss self-
identity and bonding in the remainder of this chapter, and religion and
politics in the next.

Tomas and Michael

The Polish American father and son illustrated the effects of rock 'n'
roll on family efforts to develop self-identity among children. Tomas is a
sixty-one-year-old accountant and real estate broker. He emigrated from
Poland to Houston in 1973, and completed high school there. He is hard
working, upwardly mobile, and a leader in the Polish American community. He and his American-born wife have two sons: Michael who is a
high school student and Francis who is in elementary school. Tomas and
Michael have contrasting views of rock 'n' roll's place in Michael's life—
the videotaped conversation brought out these tensions quite nicely.

We began the conversation with Tomas describing how important
rock 'n' roll was in his travels to America. He started high school in
Poland as a typical rock music fan there: he enjoyed British groups like
the Who, German groups like the Scorpions, and American groups like
the Beach Boys. His appreciation of mainstream rock 'n' roll was a great
resource for becoming an American high school student:

> My English wasn't all that strong. I did not know much about
> American history. But, you know, I knew their (American students')
> music and liked their bands. I traded tapes from Europe with them—
> the Polish tapes had different songs on them (than the American stu-
> dents had heard). I was one of them.

When I shifted attention to Michael, he relayed an expected identity of a
junior in Catholic high school who was lead singer for a punk garage
band. I attended one of their concerts at McGregor's, a music club in
Houston that caters to local bands on Friday evenings, you know, five
bands, five bucks, but you rarely get to see the same bands stay together
for the gig next week. In any event, the dark downstairs room was populated by three audience groups: friends from St. George High school,
giggling and cheering girls from St. Mary's High School, and proud middle-class parents lining the back wall to proudly videotape their sons on
the family camcorder. Michael focused his attention during the interview
on the music, what struck me as Green Day kind-of punk with meaningful lyrics. When his dad offered a positive comparison with Green Day,
Michael quickly responded: "No, dad, they (Green Day) are way too
poppy."

Michael then gave me a tour of his room: a First Holy Communion
Rosary draped across a CD storage case; numerous certificates and med-

als for honor roll and National Honor Society successes, and about a half dozen rock band posters on the walls.

At this point, Tomas proudly informed me of Michael's band's competitive success. They were finalists for a "Battle of the Bands" show at McGregor's to take place the following weekend. Michael became visibly uneasy hearing his father brag about him as if he were in a spelling bee. Michael soon broke in and said: "Dad, it's not the competition that's real, it's the music." Michael felt that his father demeaned him as being a mere child accomplishing child-like things, as opposed to appreciating him as an autonomous adult artist.

Although Tomas and Michael perceived rock 'n' roll's place in their family differently, it served as a medium to relate to each other. Their separate interpretations are vivid indicators of what they expect of each other and themselves. Tomas used rock 'n' roll to illustrate just how gifted and successful his son is. Michael used rock 'n' roll to illustrate just how different he is from his father—but not in any seriously bad way that would disrupt the essence of his good relationship with his father.

Mildred and Francine

Mildred and Francine illustrate a distinctive gender difference I discovered in my study. Whereas fathers and sons will occasionally disagree/argue over taste in music, mothers and daughters seem a bit more likely to share tastes in music. The women in my study generally felt that pop music brought them closer together. Mildred is a sixty-two-year-old Anglo sales associate, and her daughter Francine is a university student. Mildred notes that Francine has become her best friend ever since her husband left her about five years ago, and music has been a key feature of that bonding experience:

> Francine and I always liked the same singers and groups. . . . even the dumb children's music she liked from TV, what was it, *Sesame Street*. When Rob left me, she was so sweet—she told me old Beatles music was a good way to handle being sad.

Like many Anglo women her age, country music has become a very rewarding style of pop music—and rock 'n' roll specifically. Country music fits her generation, her gender, her relationships with men, her evolving aesthetics, and her relationship with her daughter:

> There's a lot of rock 'n' roll in country, as everyone knows. I never was aware of that when I was younger . . . who would have thought that Elvis was a country singer at heart? Country's great because it fits who I am. I like to dance, and I like to go out with the girls. George Strait and Alan Jackson are the kind of good-looking men I might even run across. . . Country songs talk about adult relationships, good and bad— not puppy love.

Francine described the way the country music has helped her become a "girlfriend" with her mom:

> You know where to find me and mom in March: The Houston (Live-stock Show and) Rodeo. I bet we go to five or six shows together. This year, we saw Keith Urban, who's kinda country rock, Brad Paisley, who's a babe, and Sugarland. . . . Right, that's what great about the Rodeo: we get to see really popular singers like the Black Eyed Peas, who are more hip hop than anything else.

In summary, the interviews were interesting sociologically for two other reasons. First, I learned that although parents and children can share music experiences—popular as well as school and church music—they do not always talk about these shared experiences. This phenomenon may be a corollary of the fact that art is primarily ascetic, often ineffable, and the kind of experience that does not requires language to appreciate (Storr 1992). Second, shared music seems most pleasurable when there is no other reason for sharing music beside the pleasure itself. When shared music is introduced into other micro-political situations (e.g., establishing family status), it can lose its magic for the parents and child.

FIVE

The Believing and Political Selves: Religion and Sax in the White House

As we have seen, baby boomers' early experiences of rock 'n' roll music were complex. They learned to love, play, and develop a sense of self through the idiom. They also used rock 'n' roll as a resource for meaning, as a medium for assembling their personal philosophies of life. Although the counterculture heavily critiqued the beliefs of the older generations, it provided the basis for establishing two self-experiences: a believing self and a political self. These experiences are not the same as the use of rock 'n' roll to socialize children as we have seen above. Here, I am focusing on the genesis and evolution of the parents' own beliefs about life and the world(s) beyond one's own self.

RELIGION (AND SPIRITUALITY)

Rock 'n' roll has long influenced spirituality among its fans (Seay and Neely 1986). In adulthood, the spiritual dimension of rock 'n' roll continues to impact the self as spiritual or religious believer. The lyrics and mood created by such performers as Van Morrison ("Astral Weeks") and U2 ("The Joshua Tree") provide baby boomers with nonsectarian yet religion-friendly soundtracks. New Age Music, such as that produced by Windham Hill, and recent recordings of Gregorian Chants, "Music for Paradise" by the Cistercian monks of Stift Heiligenkreuz in Germany function much the same way.

Rock 'n' roll music has also had direct influence on spirituality by helping shape organized religious ceremonies and rituals to fit the adults' tastes. For example, Catholic baby boomers grew up at a time when the Church, largely as a result of the Vatican II Council, encouraged parishes to make use of local musical styles and talent. Witness the emergence of the rock 'n' roll mass in the 1970s. Today, the very popular style of praise and worship music, with its electronic keyboard and modern melodies, is permeating Catholic liturgy.

As baby boomers age, there is a tendency among them to return to organized religion. Some of that movement is obviously fueled by being married, having children, responding to pressure from grandparents, and so forth. This movement coincides with attempts among many church leaders to modernize liturgies, ministries, and relationships with the faithful (Roof 1999). The Catholic Church, for example, has shifted emphasis from medieval ecclesiastic music to more popular styles of music, thus raising the questions of authenticity I am discussing throughout this book. In the debate over the appropriateness of popular church music theological concerns often emerge. I will now briefly discuss the issue of authenticity relating to two recent styles of music permeating Catholic worship: praise and worship music and the Christian singer-songwriter.

Praise and Worship Music

Praise and worship music originated in the youth-oriented Jesus Movement of the 1960s and 1970s (Scheer 2006). The young people involved in this Southern California-originated movement were seeking an alternative, a timely and user-friendly way to celebrate the basic Christian beliefs with which they were raised. Over time, this festive, exciting, upbeat musical style became integrated with the larger Christian music industry, and came to be known as praise and worship music. This style has been very interdenominational in scope, and has gained great popularity by its use of contemporary instrumentation (e.g., amplified band instruments, keyboards, and guitars) and links with the pop music industry (e.g., concern with charts, producers, recording companies, sales, and marketing). The songs continue to be an upbeat blending of lyrics derived from both the Old and New Testaments. Major stars include Amy Grant and Michael W. Smith.

Discussions over authenticity in praise and worship music tend to focus less on the status of any particular songs than on the validity of the genre itself. Is praise and worship music really (authentic) Christian music? In terms of the sociological ways I am framing my argument, the answers focus specifically on the contrasting ways popular Church music may impact the spiritual self of the faithful. The proponents of praise and worship music clearly feel that any style of music that brings people closer to the Lord is authentic. The detractors, however, argue that the musical style itself is consequential and cannot be accepted arbitrarily.

Take Danielle, for example, a fifty-eight year-old music and choir director for a Catholic Parish. She has seen the styles of music shift greatly in the Church, beginning with Latin-based psalms in the 1950s, to the first

English-language songs in the 1960s, to rock masses in the 1970s, to the open-horizon of styles resulting from the praise and worship movement. For her, the issue of authenticity has shifted over time, just as the music has evolved. Her original position on changing musical styles matched that of the opponents of popular Church music: the style of music is the true object of evaluation and control, even more than any particular song, artist, or lyric in question. As an illustration, Danielle approached praise and worship music in much the same way critics (e.g., the Parents' Music Resource Center) approached heavy metal music in the 1980s (Kotarba 1994). For Danielle and other senior music directors in the Church, authentic praise and worship music is that which is not confounded by a "star system." By star system, Danielle is referring to the egocentered careers of some Christian music performers "who put themselves above their music and the good message they should want to convey." Therefore, for Danielle and other baby boomer musicians, authenticity in Christian music is synonymous with, parallel to, and performed into being by the humility of the performer and performance.

Danielle's experience illustrates how adult opponents of popular Church music are leery of the negative (read: sinful) effects the overall secular and materialist architecture of popular Church music can have on the souls (read: selves) of the faithful. Danielle's ministry may be typical insofar as her choir and musical ensemble will perform praise and worship songs without even mention of the "star" Christian artist who either composed the song or made it popular. Her more recent experiences of popular Church music allow for commercial considerations that are acceptable because they (ironically) enable singer-songwriters to teach messages of humility, simplicity, and traditional spiritualism to an audience increasingly hungry for them—but they prefer to hear these messages on CDs (Kotarba 2008). Her favorite contemporary Christian musician is John Michael Talbot.

John Michael Talbot: A Postmodern, Catholic, Baby Boomer Troubadour

John Michael Talbot's music is an exemplar of authentic, contemporary, Catholic/Christian music for people of faith like Danielle. Talbot is an American Roman Catholic singer-guitarist who is also the founder of a monastic community: the Brothers and Sisters of Charity (Talbot 1999). He is the largest selling Catholic musical artist ever with over four million albums sold. He has authored or coauthored fifteen books. John Michael tours through the United States in support of his monastic community nestled in the beautiful Ozark Mountains in Arkansas. On the surface, John Michael appears much like the high profile artists about whom Danielle is cautious. John Michael Talbot is authentic to his followers, however, because he leads a simple lifestyle and does not personally profit from his talent and dedication. In a very postmodern way, John

Michael is able to integrate his Internet site, concert tours, and many followers into a pristine, humble, and monastic lifestyle that will never make the cover of People magazine. His persona is refreshing—and authentic—to those baby boomers who are a bit overwhelmed by mass-mediated culture, even of an ecclesiastic sort.

According to his biographer, Bernard Baur, John Michael Talbot's spiritual journey can be traced back to the early 1970s, when he was an eighteen-year-old rock 'n' roller (Baur 2011). He was a member of the popular country rock band, Mason Proffit, that toured with such famous performers as the Byrds, Pink Floyd, and even the Grateful Dead. After performing at the Ozark Mountain Folk Fair in Eureka Springs, Arkansas in 1973, John Michael had an epiphany. He realized that drugs, alcohol, and other lifestyle excesses on, behind, and in front of the stage were not all they were cracked up to be:

> "Suddenly," he recalls, "the rock star life seemed empty and sad. It wasn't at all what I wanted my life to stand for." It was a prophetic experience for the youngster that caused him to question his whole lifestyle as he began to ask, "Isn't there something more?" . . . Up to that point he had rubbed shoulders with the rock stars he admired and emulated. He shared stages and dressing rooms with them, which gave him an insider's view of the rock scene. After meeting some of his heroes and seeing how they really lived their lives, Talbot came to an inescapable conclusion. "There were some real tragic scenarios being played out," he says, "and it caused me to stop cold and do some serious thinking." (Baur 2011)

John Michael left the band to seek a more spiritual lifestyle. For four years, he explored Native American religions, Hinduism, Judaism, Buddhism, and Fundamentalism. He joined the Jesus Movement and examined all the Christian denominations. He concluded that Catholicism was the path for him.

John Michael felt impelled to use his particular talent to experience the ascetic. He believes that sacred music is sacramental and:

> from an arts perspective, both reflects and guides the faithful. That music, based on faith, can take the listener on a closer walk with God, actually taking them into the heart of the Lord. "It brings out the mysterious and speaks the unspeakable, bringing to light that which is beyond human reason." "Furthermore," he says, "the role of music and prayer fulfills a prophetic function. Not that musicians are prophets," he notes, "but they do have an obligation to lead." (Baur 2011)

John Michael embarked on a career that to date has produced over forty musical recordings and four million album sales. In 1982, he was the recipient of the prestigious Dove Award for Worship Album of the Year, *Light Eternal*, with producer and longtime friend, Phil Perkins. Four years later, he became one of only nine artists to receive the President's Merit

Award from the National Academy of Recording Arts and Sciences and in 1988 he was named the No. 1 Christian Artist by *Billboard* magazine.

John Michael performs at fifty or so live concerts a year, largely at parish church venues around the country. I attended four performances: at St. Thomas More Church in Houston; at the dramatic Catholic Charismatic Center in Houston, at an intimate private chapel in suburban Houston; and at the Dominican Center in San Antonio, Texas. The suburban performance was part of a three-evening event that included collective prayer, quiet meditation, and lecture/discussion of the common spiritual links among the various belief systems around the world. The chapel is a beautiful structure designed after the Byzantium architectural style of early Christianity. The audience was smaller—one hundred or so—than the larger audiences that fill the naves of modern parish churches. In contrast to the mix of families, couples, and individuals common to the larger concerts, this group was comprised mostly of couples. The attendees appeared very professional and prosperous. They were dressed in crisply pressed Dockers, modest skirts, and nice leather sandals.

The attendees were very much from the baby boomer generation. In conversations with a number of them, I learned that they in general felt that John Michael Talbot's ministry fulfilled several needs for them. First, his ministry is calm and positive. James is a sixty-seven-year-old retired engineer:

> I've looked forward to retirement for a long time, and I really enjoy surrounding myself with the quiet, as I read somewhere. John Michael's music fits the bill.

Second, his music is enjoyable and accessible. Robert and Agnes have been married for thirty-seven years. He is an attorney and she is a retired accountant. They compared Talbot's music to the secular music they prefer:

> We have always liked singer-songwriter music. One of our first dates was to see Neil Young do an acoustic set. With John Michael, you get the good music that's good or you (laugh).

Third, he is much like his audience, in a number of ways, most important of which is being a Catholic. Catherine is a middle-age, single woman who fancies herself a spiritual seeker and experimenter:

> I'm like a lot of people in our generation. Ever since the '60s, I've played with Buddhism, Tao, Siddha Yoga mediation, Protestantism—you name it. Let's face it . . . a lot of people raised Catholic have given up their faith to find the personal and comfortable experiences John Michael Talbot provides. It's great—and you don't have to convert to another religion or anything!

In interview, John Michael related to me that this audience was typical insofar as it consisted of people who adhere to a range of religious and

spiritual beliefs: Protestants, agnostics, Buddhists, Jews, and others, all
with one particular need:

> They love the music. For some, it serves as a pathway to find a way. For
> others who have found a way for themselves, the music helps make the
> journey along that path pleasant, meaningful, and relevant.

John Michael Talbot is an archetypical baby boomer: postmodern, yet
traditional, yet experimental. He is able to navigate through what might
appear to be numerous religious and spiritual contradictions without
compromising his commitment to and acceptance by the formal Roman
Catholic Church. For example, his music is very eclectic by integrating
rock, folk, ecclesiastic, classical, chant, early church music and the music
of the Medieval and Renaissance eras. He uses the funds generated by his
music to support a monastic community that include married as well as
single people, The Brothers and Sisters of Charity at Little Portion Hermi-
tage. All commit to vows of poverty, chastity, and obedience. His ministry is open to all, but he has also shared his music with Pope John Paul II
and Mother Theresa (Baur 2011). His ministry is timeless, yet the infra-
structure is state-of-the art recording and Internet communications. The
message is simple, and the media are complex, yet the encouragement to
followers is to engage in spiritual readings, vigils fasting and manual
labor. All this is a nice alternative—escape?—for the busy suburban tech-
nocrat who wants to have it both ways. As one attendee at the chapel
performance put it, he never thought he would be able to listen to—and
actually enjoy—Catholic music on a CD in his car on the way to the
office.

Lonnie and Celine

Lonnie and Celine were respondents in my "Our Parents' Music"
study. Lonnie is a sixty-one-year-old African American university administrator and her daughter, Celine, is an attorney. Pop music is woven
through just about every aspect of their relationship. Church music is the
key feature here. They have grown up together as both participants and
fans of Christian pop music. Lonnie traced this shared celebration back to
singing in the choir:

> I remember the first Sunday we took Celine to Church. She was just a
> baby, but clapped her hands along with the music. I knew I had a choir
> partner just then. . . . She just loved the children's choir. In fact, our
> Church had several choirs—we all loved to sing the praises of our
> Lord.

The great variety of gospel and spiritual music in the African American
Church fueled an ongoing love for the evolution of gospel and spiritual
styles. Celine mentioned Kirk Franklin as someone they share, yet at the
cutting edge of gospel music:

> We saw Kirk Franklin together at the Hobby Theater downtown. Some women like him because he is so handsome and sensual. We like him because he can sing the praises of the Lord while still looking good and being a true man.

Celine likes many varieties of music, not all of which are apparently conducive to being a faithful believer. Lonnie defends Celine's eclectic tastes because they remind her of her tastes in music when she was younger:

> When I was growing up, we liked Motown and some of that was pretty sexy for its day. Hip hop is alright, or at least some of it is. Music is music and it's all good. They even had a Christian hip hop dance group at church awhile back and they were great. . . . There are many ways to honor the Lord.

Thus, the baby boomer taste if not search for spiritual enlightenment can include a range of musical styles and experiences. The difference between religious and secular music can get pretty blurry.

THE POLITICAL SELF: SAX IN THE WHITE HOUSE

Rock 'n' roll music serves as a soundtrack for situations in which baby boomers perceive themselves as political actors. Rock 'n' roll can add both atmosphere and meaning to political events. For example, New York punk poet and singer Patti Smith performed a concert in Houston on March 28, 2003, right at the beginning of the war in Iraq. The concert was originally scheduled simply to support an exhibit of her art displayed at the Museum of Contemporary Arts. The audience was overwhelmingly composed of middle-age people, dressed up in their good jeans and long (hippie) skirts. Through conversations with numerous fans after the concert, it was clear that they enjoyed the concert. Patti Smith's poetry and songs (e.g., "People Have the Power") gave them a relevant and identifiable venue for sharing their overwhelmingly negative feelings about the war.

Musical inauthenticity can also serve as a powerful interactional tool in establishing one's political acumen as correct and one's political self as astute. If one's political opponent appreciates bad, inappropriate—or inauthentic—music, the very persona of that opponent can be discredited, to his or her political disadvantage. A recent example of this phenomenon was the media coverage to a survey inquiring as to the 2008 U.S. presidential candidates' musical preferences. One could almost predict the differences between Barack Obama's and John McCain's music (www.obama-mccain.info/compare-obama-mccain-music.php).   Since McCain is a member of the baby boomer generation, there is no surprise in learning that his favorite style of music is 1950s and 1960s rock 'n' roll.

He is also a big fan of ABBA, and recently purchased a CD, *The Very Best of the Beach Boys*. Again, predictably, Obama's taste in music is much more eclectic, matching the tastes of the Generation X of which he is a member (e.g., Miles Davis, Bob Dylan, Stevie Wonder, Bach, and the Fugees). Whereas Obama's conservative critics lambasted him for pandering to his youthful and therefore unsophisticated supporters, McClain's liberal critics used his choices in music as evidence that he is old and out of touch with today's styles and values. The often heated discussion among baby boomers of candidates' musical tastes and preferences should not be surprising. This is the generation of music fans that learned to attach their very basic sense of self to musical performers and styles as adolescents and young adults. I simply ask the middle-age and aging reader to recall those frequent debates in the dorm or in the club on who is better, the (pop-oriented) Beatles or the (hard rocker) Rolling Stones? The beat goes on.

Peter and Ben

Peter and Ben love to argue over two things: music and politics. Sometimes the two topics intertwine. I interviewed them at an appropriate location: a rally in favor of Palestinian rights in the Middle East. Peter is a sixty-one-year-old university professor and Ben is a freshman in college. Their family culture encourages debate, discussion, and argumentation at home. Peter and Ben often make sense of current political events by interpreting them through music, the music industry, and music history.

Take the current, ongoing American war(s) in the Middle East. Peter uses pop music to examine the apparent lack of serious resistance to the conflict here in the United States:

> There is no viable anti-war movement. Our society has turned into a dying empire constantly fighting wars to protect its colonies. There is no antiwar music like we had in World War II and in Vietnam? Why not? The music industry will not put up with a truly viable alternative music industry that will preach against the war and divert profits away from the major labels.

Ben sees another side to the story and makes sure his dad hears it:

> Dad, we would have an anti-war culture today if your generation didn't kill it off with drugs and other excesses of your countercultural generation. Don't forget, your legacy to us is disco.

Now, that hurts!

ROCK 'N' ROLL AND POLITICS IN THE TWENTY-FIRST CENTURY

My argument about the important political role of rock 'n' roll music for adults might end here if we did not take into consideration the progeny of rock ' n' roll, specifically hip hop and rap. As I argued earlier, rock 'n' roll has been an important influence on the emergence and growth of rap music as a cultural force in our society. Rap was born in the late 1970s and early 1980s largely as a medium for young minority people's political issues and statements. Grandmaster Flash and NWA easily come to mind as prime examples of rappers with political messages. Well, the very earliest rap fans are now aging adults. And, rap music is among the most global of all popular music forms (Tate 2003). Other societies have fairly long histories of adults enjoying rock 'n' roll alongside their children, for example, Poland and Germany (Kotarba 2002b). Rap music is following a similar process, but on more of a shared, global basis.

The example in point is a very recent one. In the course of the political uprisings in the Middle East, specifically Egypt, the insurgency has been largely communicated and coordinated through the Internet and over cell phones. The soundtrack for the insurgency in Egypt has been rap music. Although the assumption was made early on by Western journalists and other observers that Egyptian youth were in the forefront in this regard, we are learning that adult insurgents also experienced rap revolutionary songs—produced in Egypt—as motivation and meaning for the revolution.

Political communication online takes place on easy to construct homepages. For example, "Mideastune" is a repository for political messages in Egypt, but also for messages that have apparently been influential in Yemen, Bahrain, Iran, and other political hotspots in early 2011 (http://mideastunes.com/egypt-fight-song-behead-the-king/). Among other links is a video, *Behead the King*, produced almost immediately during the early days of the uprising in the streets of Alexandria and Cairo, with video clips taken by cell phone cameras and clips sampled from CNN. What is interesting in this postmodern turn of events is that we increasingly witness adults depending on youth-generated media for political communications and motivation. I will revisit the emergence of rap music in Middle Eastern politics in chapter nine in my concept of *hybrid scene*.

SIX

The Integrated Self: KLM Flight #0661

One of the most noteworthy features of the late adult segment of the lifecycle is the felt need to tie it all together.[6] Eric Erickson (1993) referred to this experience as "wisdom & renunciation," in which the person seeks calmness, tolerance, appropriate emotional detachment, peace of mind, and universal reconciliation. Making sense of life is more than managing one event or crisis after another, as is the case in mid-adulthood. In our culture, the older one gets, the more one seeks unity in one's experience of life. Religion is a common tool to help do this. Among baby boomers in our society, the music they grew up with can serve the same purpose. Rock 'n' roll is one of the constants in their lives. Popular tastes change, instrumentation changes, media change, and performance venues change. But the music is always there and can literally serve as a sound-track for one's life.

There are certain occasions when music serves to tie it all together. These situations are common in everyday life, and can trigger a sense of past, present, and future. The following is an account of just that type of occasion in my life (Kotarba 2005). The text below is excerpted from an experience of self-exploration and definition that occurred when return-ing from a trip to Europe. I was invited to lecture at the University of Aalborg in Denmark. My wife accompanied me, and we were tourists for several days. We traveled around Denmark and Sweden by train, and had a great time with our Scandinavian friends. Our return flight on KLM departed from Amsterdam at 10 a.m. on a bright and sunny day. I surfed the KLM in-flight magazine for entertainment options, and the "Showcase: California Dreaming," with Paul Sexton, caught my atten-tion. After the first song was played, I felt like this could be a very valu-able experience for my research on baby boomer rock 'n' roll fans. I pulled out my laptop and proceeded to create a Word file containing all

my thoughts, feelings, and conversation related to the program as I listened to it. In this regard, my method differed from autoethnography
(Ellis 2002) because I was not analytical in my note taking. My notes were
literal, not literary. I was thinking out loud into my computer, so to
speak.

The program lasted about one hour. When I got home, I quickly con-
tacted KLM Flight Services to try to obtain the program on disk. I wanted
a complete song list and the exact script followed by Paul Sexton in
making his commentary on the historical, biographical, and musicological roots of 1960s California pop music. They referred my request to
"Inflight Productions" in London, who sent me the complete program on
two compact disks. The following experience occurred as the clouds
passed as steady as an hourglass.

(The text in **bold** is conversation with my wife. Normal text is internal
and private interaction with myself. Explanatory and interpretive statements are in parentheses.)

> March 26 2005 . . . 11:10 a.m. . . . somewhere over the North Sea . . . My
> wife, Polly, and I are returning to Houston from a trip to Denmark and
> Sweden. . . . The soundtrack for this segment of my life is an audio
> music program called "Showcase: California Dreaming," with Paul
> Sexton. I have never heard of him, so I assume he is a regular announc-
> er who reads scripts for these kinds of programs.
>
> Wow, the plane is really packed! I can't believe we got two seats by
> the window . . . pays to do all that shit on line.
>
> Free headphones. Why did I bother to pack two sets I got free that
> last time I flew? Let's see, it looks like we're gonna see a Renée Zell-
> weger movie. Is that the best Katy, Texas can offer? She's too weird for
> a movie star, at least in this movie.
>
> Forget the movie. This is like a *Seinfeld* episode. (A very large man
> sits in two adjacent seats four rows ahead of me, blocking my view of
> the video screen.)
>
> **Where do you plug these things in** (I ask my wife about the ear-
> buds)? **You gonna watch Renee? I hate her.**
>
> Ah, a little elevator music. Always soothing to the soul. All these in-
> flight programs are choreography for the clouds. Is that Air Supply?
>
> A little classical stuff. A gift from my kids (all three of our children
> are accomplished musicians: jazz saxophone, flute and clarinet). **When
> is Andrew's concert** (I ask my wife regarding his spring symphony
> concert at the University of Michigan)? **Are you sure it's not this com-
> ing week?**
>
> The *New York Times* on board? Cool . . . we're not even stopping in
> New York. Article on electronic gadgets. I should get an iPod? I gotta
> look into the Blackberry, although I cannot afford one and I'm not sure
> what I would do with one.
>
> Let's see, channel four. Some program called California Dreamin'?
> Mamas and Papas. "California Dreaming." Let's see, I was a sopho-
> more. St. Procopius College, on the radio, in my dorm room. It was in

the new men's dorm, I had good grades and was able to escape the three-bed old dorm. It was a sunny but cold February day in Illinois. What was California then? . . . I had no idea.

I gotta email Michael when we get back. What a great host. He really got into the CDs I brought him. Thank you messages to Lars (Department Chair at Aalborg who will be a visitor at Indiana University in fall 2005)? Why not? I have to send him info on Sally (my wife's cousin who lives in Bloomington, Indiana) like I promised him. That trip was better than I could have planned. Danes are really nice people, not cold or distant at all. Where was all the Danish death metal I expected to hear? I guess we did not spend enough time with students.

Good airplane food, uh? Look at this . . . real meat.

The Byrds playing "Mr. Tambourine Man." Too slick to compete with the Beatles. "Mr. Tambourine Man." Roger McGuinn says the Byrds were electrified before Dylan. I don't know about that. Sounds like hype for Roger.

It looks like land down there. Scotland? Are there hills like that in Scotland?

Polly, they're playing the Airplane. (Polly puts on her earphones and puts a real smile on her face.) I know she loves Gracie Slick. Polly's kind of like an old hippie. No, she is an old hippie. Don't all old hippies get married and have kids and buy houses? Gracie Slick's a bad girl. Are all old hippies bad girls? I don't think so.

Polly and I are enjoying Bailey's and coffee. Nice drink for old hippies like us. . . a little coffee to keep us awake, and a little booze to make us mellow.

Jim Morrison and the Doors. Ray Manzarek talks about meeting Jim on the beach. Robbie Kreiger wrote the songs. His very first song was "Light My fire." One of the first long songs of the sixties. Wow, great stuff . . . who is this guy, Sexton?

Ray again. Jim and Van Morrison jamming together to "Gloria" at the Whisky a Go Go. "The End." I really have to put that piece on Van in my book. Van's hard to figure out. He doesn't sing that well. His music is cool—good blues. But you find what you want sifting through his music.

First Grateful Dead song. Too bad the Dead only made it to Houston once. John (my brother-in-law who lives in Oregon) would come down again for any kind of Dead reunion. God gave us brothers-in-law for specific reasons. Some are experts on income taxes. Some are family leaders. John is my music bro.

By 1968, the West Coast sound was getting harder. Blue Cheer. Man, we were still listening to Motown and folk back in Illinois. Were we behind times, or were they ahead of the times? Willie Arduino (freshman at Illinois State University back in 1969) was cool. . . God, his skit at the Fourth Floor Fine Arts Forum was great (in the dorm at ISU) . . . Country Joe and the Fish. I would love to see him again.

Folk singer songwriter movement came at the disillusioned end of the California movement. CSN. Davis Crosby interview: "Music is magic . . ."

Why so many love songs in the '60s? "Suite Judy Blues Eyes." Crosby, Stills and Nash . . . Powerful love song! I think we look back to the
sixties and think we see only anti-war, depression, and drugs. Why did
the hippie-types need relationship songs?

Good pop. Mama Cass Eliot. "It's getting better." Perfect ending.

Is Renee over yet? I wanna see the *Johnson Family Vacation*.

REFLECTIONS

There was nothing special or unusual about the flight. My wife and I
looked forward to the long flight as an opportunity to relax after a very
busy and exciting trip. The flight did, however, provide the occasion for a
common experience for upper-middle-age men like me. A musical program served as a suggestive musical template for conducting the internal
and external dialogues that comprise the experience of self.

When the musical program began and the first song—the Beach Boys'
version of "Summertime Blues," originally recorded by Eddie Cochran in
the 1950s—was playing, I thought it might be fun to keep track of my
thoughts as I listened to the Grateful Dead, Beach Boys, Mamas & Papas,
Jefferson Airplane, Jim Morrison, and so forth. I pulled out my laptop
and created a transcript of my thoughts and feelings while listening to
the program. So much of my life—who I was and who I am—is tied to
this music.

The existential model of the self I introduced in chapter 1 provides a
useful analytical tool for understanding this experience. Jack Douglas
proposed the idea of an existential self in the mid-1970s to account for the
increasingly obvious way people's sense of who they are is in a state of
constant change. People experience the self as becoming, yet as Douglas
notes, it never arrives at a state of certainty, even in adulthood:

> (The members of society) recognize that we are commonly only vague-
> ly defined, that we are often conflictfully defined, that sometimes we
> are terrifyingly unclear about who or what we are, even when others
> are able to give us a clear set of definitions in terms of our complex
> involvement in (institutionalized) role play. They often recognize that
> we are able to re-create ourselves, but that doing so is a difficult, nonra-
> tionalizable activity with uncertain outcome. They increasingly recog-
> nize that who we are, what we are, is continuously in the process of
> becoming and that we ourselves, though able to affect the outcomes of
> the process of becoming through our continual struggles, are not able
> to dictate the outcomes of this flux. (Douglas 1984: 96)

The present exercise is a direct attempt to answer the following question:
How do upper middle-age adults use popular music to cultivate a sense
of self? The answer is that actively engaging the process of the becoming
of self can be as rewarding—or more rewarding—as actually achieving a

goal or model of self. A simple example is weight and weight loss in our culture. The explicit goal for many is to be a fit, skinny, or thin person and to self-define as such. This goal is reinforced—if not generated—by the mass media. The payoff for sense of self for many people, though, comes primarily from making the *commitment* (Sartre 1945) to losing weight and working to accomplish the ultimate goal of getting thin and fit.

Who we are is largely a function of trying to find out who we are. We tend to be relatively satisfied with who we are—at least for the moment—when the process of becoming itself makes sense. This is the way popular music feeds into the process. Baby Boomers are likely to have used this idiom to answer specific questions related to self: intimate relationships, conflict with parents and other authority figures, personal style, peers, etc. As adults, however, being a rock 'n' roll fan in itself has rewards for the self. Appreciating the KLM Flight #0661 program aesthetically, technologically, nostalgically, and autobiographically, for example, can give one a sense of security, relevance, belonging, continuity, and style.

Annotated comments on my in-flight experience include the following themes:

Framework for recalling and putting closure on the just completed trip to Denmark. I was able to consider my trip in terms of the music I experienced there, as well as the music that was expected but not performed.

Locating the self historically. Music reminds me that my self is an extended experience, but one that undergoes different priorities, contingencies and meanings.

Interpreting my wife. The music I heard gave me great pleasure by proving me glimpses into the past, where my wife was very current, playful, and loving. The resulting feeling is a good one, since my wife is essentially the same person now as she was then. How do I know that? My wife enjoys the same music.

Appreciating current friends. My gift of music was a great way to solidify a pleasurable and growing friendship. Everyone likes music.

Passing time on a long flight. Music is a great way to pass time. One can be very passive and relaxed by letting the music create reality.

Reminder of other current agenda items. The music played helped organize my day and activities.

SEVEN

The Sociable Self and the Blues

There is a paradox in the musical socialization of baby boomers. On the one hand, baby boomers comprise the generation that experienced rapid developments in the quality and extent of the mechanical reproduction of popular music (Benjamin 1936). I received my first record in 1957, Elvis's "Love Me Tender." Purchasing that record was a major family adventure. My father drove my sister Maryann and me to Andy Senak's Record Store on Pulaski Road on Chicago's south side. The record was a beautiful thing: a heavy object with that elegant RCA Victor label in the middle. My rock 'n' roll armamentarium quickly shifted to 45 singles, 33 albums, 8 tracks, cassettes, CDs, MP3s, DVDs, and downloads of various kinds. Needless to say, AM radio quickly led to FM, satellite, and now Internet radio and Pandora. The music industry seemed hell-bent on assembling an audio world that would provide me with pop music no matter where I was—but increasingly to an audience of one.

The paradox appears when we realize that my generation was provided perhaps the most opportunity ever to enjoy live music of various kinds. We had sock hops, concerts, clubs, school music programs, and increasingly contemporary church music. We were the generation that rallied around itself—while indulging itself—at the infamous outdoor rock music festival. Where were you during Woodstock?

My point is that rock 'n' roll music served as one of the key features of our distinctive style of sociability. Georg Simmel (1950) wrote about sociability as that aspect of our everyday lives through which we engage others in fairly inconsequential and primarily enjoyable interaction. Sociability does not ordinarily involve survival, political or economic goals, although these consequential phenomena can be related. In the 1960s and 1970s, our patterns of sociability expanded into live music as we spent less and less time at the movies or even in front of the television. Our college years were especially defined by live music, as were our dating experiences. Estelle is a sixty-one-year-old investment banker who attended the University of Texas in Austin during the Cosmic Cowboy era. She recalls spending many weekend evenings on 6th Street with her dorm mates:

> We'd go to Antones and the Continental Club, places like that. The music was wonderful. Artists like Willie Nelson, Ray Wylie Hubbard, Jerry Jeff Walker were regulars on stage—no big deal. It was OK to just be with the girls, no hassles.

Sometimes the girls would go their own way:

> There'd be there or four of us, but one of us would see a guy she knew—or would like to know—and go drink beer with him. If you'd meet a guy in a club, you usually went back to that same club for your first "real" date.

My (soon to be) wife Polly relocated to Tempe, Arizona in January 1974 to be with me. I was in the middle of my M.A. program at ASU. We took the train from the deep snow of Chicago to the deep snow of Flagstaff, then drove down to the warm sunshine of the desert. The celebration for our successful voyage? We immediately drove out to the Big Surf Water Park in Tempe to see Dave Mason (formerly of *Traffic*) in concert. Outdoor rock concert in Arizona in January? Is there a better reason to move there from Chicago?

As baby boomers survived the 1960s and 1970s, many kept their taste for live music, but increasingly on their own maturing terms. Sharing live music with a spouse, date, or friends requires comfort in advancing middle age. Instead of sharing a joint, they now share a bottle of wine in the "Gold Circle" of front row (padded, $300) seats at the (shaded) summer music shed. To share live music with friends may involve dinner and a show at an acoustic venue. Nationally, the House of Blues serves this function. In Houston, the Mucky Duck functions the same way. Julius is a sixty-three-year-old oil field supply salesman who fits live rock 'n' roll into his busy businessman's schedule:

> I take a lot of my clients to the Mucky Duck. I know, it's business, but if a guy shares your taste in music, he's a friend. You get to hear big names up close . . . I took a client who was from Dallas to see Robin Trower, and was he impressed! A great concert and a business expense.

BABY BOOMER AS FRIEND

As one enters adulthood, the self-identity of friend becomes difficult to maintain. This is especially the case among men, whose hectic and fragmented everyday lifestyle does not always leave space for the kinds of friendships typical of childhood and adolescence. Sure, middle-age and middle-class men have business associates, bosses, subordinates, golf partners, and neighbors. But friendships do not always get the time and personal investment needed to thrive.

ROCK 'N' ROLL FOR JOINERS: THE BLUES SCENE

There is a truism in our culture that says that some people are joiners and others are simply not. When people age in our society, and eventually retire for example, they generally maintain their earlier, even lifelong, styles of sociality—it is not likely that you will join let alone enjoy living in a busy retirement village if you spent your entire adulthood in front of a television (Fontana 1976). Similarly, baby boomers who experience their adolescence and early adulthood regularly sharing rock 'n' roll music with others and in the presence of others will continue to do so as they get older.

Although it has been argued that Americans are losing their traditional commitment to community involvement (Putnam 2000), the opposing case in question is the local blues society. There are numerous blues societies in cities ranging from Vancouver, Canada to Cocoa Beach, Florida. The nonprofit Blues Foundation, with headquarters in Memphis, Tennessee, claims 160 affiliated Blues organizations in the United States and around the world (http://www.blues.org). Local blues organizations are almost exclusively staffed by volunteers, and they engage in the following types of activities:

- Publication of monthly or quarterly newsletters
- Weekly or monthly blues jams in local clubs
- Special, typically seasonal, parties, picnics, or dances as fundraisers
- Benefit activities for sick or aging blues musicians, or for the families of deceased blues musicians
- Educational programs, such as "Blues in Schools" programs
- Promotional activities for local blues artists

The local blues organizations affiliated with the Blues Foundation also participate in annual competitions. The major activity in this category is the International Blues Challenge, held annually in Memphis. Local affiliates are encouraged to conduct local competitions to produce an artist or bands to represent the affiliate. A second activity is the annual Blues Music Awards:

> considered the "Blues Grammys." Blues Music Awards are the premier event for Blues professionals, musicians and fans. Held in Memphis, the focus of this celebration is to recognize superior achievements in Blues performances while honoring a cultural tradition. Each year, in conjunction with the Blues Music Awards, the Foundation also

presents the Blues Hall of Fame induction ceremony. (http://
www.blues.org/about/sponsorhandy)

Certain local blues societies occasionally conduct special activities such as
the Kentucky Blues Society's "Kentucky Blues TV," broadcast on local
public access cable television and/or the Internet. The most spectacular
local events are major blues festivals, of which there are literally dozens
annually, such as those held in Chicago, Duck Hill, Mississippi, Wilming-
ton, Delaware, and Sonora, California.

Increasingly, local blues organizations work with local or state
government arts agencies to conduct programs such as blues festivals.
Government agencies seek out these affiliations because of the growing
tourist value related to events such as music festivals.

BLUES SOCIETY MEMBERSHIP

In order to appreciate the importance of the blues to baby boomer rock 'n'
rollers, we must understand the demographic profile of the blues audience. The Blues Festival Guide is a monthly magazine geared toward
blues music fans who attend these festivals, either in their hometown as
at vacation destinations (http://www.bluesfestivalguide.com). In 2006,
the magazine conducted a survey of its readership. The data provides an
illuminating portrait of engaged blues fans. The following characteristics
are noteworthy:

> 48.2 percent are 51 years of age or older
> 66.1 percent are either married or with a significant other
> 91.2 percent are white
> 48.9 percent earn over $50,000 annually
> 75.1 percent have at least some college education
> 77 percent own their own home
> 71.6 percent purchase music CDs online
> 75.8 percent are not musicians or artists

My experience with the Houston Blues Society supports these findings.
In general, blues music fans who actively engage the blues scene are
middle-American folks. There are African Americans involved with
blues societies, but mostly as musicians, artists, producers, and club owners. Most members are white, middle-class, family-oriented, respectable,
and quiet people. The blues society appears to them to be a place where
they can meet and be with other people much like them, where they can
volunteer for fun and good causes. But, perhaps most important, they can
do all this within the context of the music they have come to love and
identify with. The sociological question now becomes: why blues music?

We all know that rock 'n' roll, and its many musical and cultural
offspring, finds their roots in blues music (Campbell 2009: 157). The field

songs, cabin songs, and folk songs of the Deep South created and sung by
Arthur Cruddup, Big Mama Thornton, and Robert Johnson in the 1940s
and 1950s were soon covered, interpreted, recorded, and popularized by
Elvis Presley and Pat Boone in the 1950s. Many musicologists, historians,
and music critics have pinpointed the features of blues music that reso-
nated strongly with post–World War II white teenagers: the embodied
freedom; the rhythm; the inconclusive and often suggestive lyrics; the
energy; the danceability, the exoticism, the resistance. I would argue that
a key feature was *electric amplification* (Kotarba 1994a). The African
American music that was originally composed in the cotton fields of
Mississippi and made its way up the mighty Mississippi River to inner-
city Memphis and Chicago was elegantly acoustic, both vocally and in-
strumentally (i.e., the guitar). Classic blues music had to be acoustic because of the expense and nonavailability of more technically advanced
acoustics. Further, classic blues music did not have to be anything but
simple and direct because the audience was small and intimate. When the
blues made its way to the big city in the 1930s and 1940s, it was performed and enjoyed in very differently kinds of venues—music clubs,
taverns, and social clubs. Perhaps more important, the audiences were
very diverse. Instead of family members and neighbors down south, the
now blues artist performed largely to fans, patrons, critics, and other
strangers. Amplification evolved to extend the music. As we move into
the 1960s, we witness that new audience of white teenagers thirsty for
music with an edge to it, something beyond the Four Freshmen sounds
their older brothers and sisters enjoyed—something loud. In a musical
cauldron brewing with ingredients ranging from Taj Mahal, Led Zeppelin, Willie Dixon, and the Rolling Stones, the blues became the dominant
rock style of the 1960s and 1970s (see also Frith 1981).

Let us fast-forward to the 2000s. We have this population bulge—
people entering their sixties—who love rock 'n' roll. But it is no longer
clear that rock 'n' roll loves them. They are a bit too old to stand all day in
the sun and heat at the rock festivals to which they hitchhiked in the
1960s. They enjoy amplified music, but not nearly as loud as they did
twenty-five years ago. (When was the last time you saw a middle-age
person glued to the Marshall Amps and speakers stack at a concert?)
They still enjoy live music, but prefer the comfort of a club to a large
concert venue. The blues easily fit the bill. What about the themes in the
blues, such as poverty, crime, discrimination, sexuality, and drugs? How
can a middle-age, middle-class white fan appreciate these things? The
answer lies in the fact that the reality portrayed by the blues is now a
historical reality. Blues fans are removed from the moral or personal responsibility for these sensitive topics. The topics belong to the past but—
like any other museum-quality phenomenon—can be explored, interpreted, and even enjoyed today (e.g., the Delta Blues Museum in Clarks-
dale, Mississippi). Phil is a sixty-one-year-old accountant who really

loves rural or field blues from the 1940s and 1950s. He uses the blues to add perspective to our modern lives and situations:

> I first learned to appreciate the blues back in the '60s. I was a Beach Boy and Johnny Cash fan until my college roommates turned me on to BB King and Blind Lemon Jefferson. I learned a lot about Black people back then. . . . The blues today remind me that those hard times are a thing of the past; we've made a lot of progress since then. But it's good to remind ourselves of what can go wrong.

Interestingly, Phil is like many other Anglo blues fans who learned of the blues from their Anglo roommates and friends.

In the remainder of this chapter, I will discuss two types of activities at the Houston Blues Society, with which I was heavily involved. These activities illustrate the ways blues societies provide members safe access to a world that is seen by them as romantic and exciting.

"BLUES-N-KIDS": THE ROLE OF THE VOLUNTEER

Given my widely known interest in popular music in Houston, Texas, I was asked to serve on the first Board of Directors of the Houston Blues Society in 1993. The board was a very interesting group. The first president of the organization was Sonny Boy Terry Jerome, a talented blues harmonica player who performed with several well-known bluesmen (e.g., Joe Hughes, Texas Johnny Brown, and Pete Mayes), and also fronted several different bands in Houston. Other board members included local music fans and promoters. Of ten total members, two were African American. We met monthly to manage such projects as weekly blues jams, a quarterly newsletter, and showcase programs at local clubs (e.g., "Women in Blues" at the Billy Blues Club in the Richmond nightclub district of Houston).

My contribution was the establishment of a "Blues-N-Kids" project that lasted three years.[7] With financial support from the Cultural Arts Council of Houston/Harris County, garage sales, fund-raising concerts, and donations, I booked local blues musicians to play and talk for one class period in schools and one hour in community centers. The ensembles ranged in size from one musician playing acoustic guitar to three- and four-member bands. Size depended on available funds and logistics. For example, I had difficulty booking full blues bands to perform during the day of or the day after a regular club or concert gig—this scheduling simply did not fit the musicians' life and work styles. The musicians were approximately 75 percent African American and 25 percent Anglo.

The format for Blues-N-Kids was intentionally informal. The musicians would play songs ranging from traditional Texas/Gulf Coast blues (e.g., Lightnin' Hopkins material) to contemporary blues (e.g., Albert Collins's and their own material). Between songs, the musicians would tell stories about their careers, the meaning of the blues, blues legends, and the relevance of the blues to the children's everyday life problems and joys. When possible, the musicians would involve the children in the music. For example, Jimmy Dotson, a guitar player and singer, composed a song about a pencil and how a student can experience the blues when the pencil breaks in the middle of a test. He would then invite students to compose their own blues lyrics to accompany a very simple and basic blues melody. Students proposed topics ranging from a girlfriend breaking up with you, to flunking a test, to having your bicycle stolen, to having your mother get very sick and being hospitalized.

The format would also vary according to the age of the audience. Very young children (5–10 years of age) liked to sing along, whereas middle- and high-school students enjoyed stories about the musicians' careers and the history of the blues in Texas. I also booked special presentations, such as a workshop on blues guitar for a guitar class at a magnet middle school for the performing arts, a workshop on blues piano for a band class at a general high school, an after-school workshop on playing the harmonica for a group of elementary school-age children at a local community center (sponsored by the Hohner Harmonica Company), and an all-female blues band performing for an African American festival at a local Catholic parish.

In all, we conducted nine presentations each of the three years of the "Blues-N-Kids" project. The project was great fun for me. I was able to hang out with a number of great blues musicians; I accomplished worthwhile community service; and I got a taste of the seductive role of the producer of culture. The project was also quite successful artistically and organizationally. The project was the major reason why the Houston Blues Society was awarded the "Keeping the Blues Alive" Award in 1996 from the Blues Heritage Society (Kotarba 1997).

My policy was to pay the musicians for their participation—I was asking them to contribute their work and their talent to our organization, which seemed fair to all involved. Nevertheless, non-profit cultural programs like "Blues-N-Kids" depend heavily on volunteers for success. The "Blues-N-Kids" project specifically made a social space for baby boomer rock 'n' roll fans. Anglo rock musicians whose careers involved success at a very local level had an opportunity to perform for pay—albeit modest—often in the presence of legendary African-American artists, who were also paid. The "Blues-N-Kids" project fit the middle-class view of teaching culture to children: rationally, in school, and with a sense of curriculum. The Blues-N-Kids project also provided the opportunity to live vicariously through "real" blues artists. We also put young and aspiring blues artists together with veteran performers.

The "Blues-N-Kids" program lasted three years. There were several reasons why it ended. The program was very labor- and time-intensive. We were unlikely to continue to receive funding from the city. We were getting a little bored. We made one mistake. We put a lot of money, time, and talent into a large number of programs directed to small audiences. We should have produced them to be recorded for multiple uses. I did videotape most of the programs, but not in a way to seriously reuse them. The main reason, however, was my effort to produce a different sort of program, one that was unique to the world of blues organizations. I sought and received funding to produce a more artistically oriented program about the blues musicians themselves. The baby boomer in question—me, the sociology professor—had the proud opportunity to serve as cultural producer.

BLACK MEN, BLACK VOICES

At the conclusion of the "Blues-N-Kids" project, I decided to change the format of my work for three reasons. First, I wanted the project to present a more complex and more relevant message to its young audiences. Specifically, the children in the audience (many of whom were African-American) were great fans of rap and rhythm as well as blues music, and most of them were raised to appreciate gospel music. After consulting with teachers, community leaders, and musicians, it seemed that a more relevant message to them would be the relationship and impact of the blues to these other styles of contemporary music. Second, the potential sociological context for this project was coming more into focus. I was not only teaching children about the blues, I was in fact helping to create the blues by creating the occasion for its performance. Third, the recently completed "Blues 'N' Schools" project was a real trip for me, a sociologist with no discernible artistic skills, but with a need to vicariously delve into the world of culture. I never thought I could ever pull off a rewarding program like "Blues-N-Kids," so I became a bit intoxicated with success. I applied for and received grants from the Texas Commission on the Arts, the National Institute for the Arts, and the Cultural Arts Council of Houston/Harris County to fund "Black Men, Black Voices."[8]

My goal was to operationalize, through live performance, a truism proclaimed by dozens of ethnomusicologists, music historians, critics, and musicians themselves: namely, that blues music and blues culture impact and inform other forms of African-American music and culture (e.g., Frith 1981). I expanded my audience to include adults representing all ethnic groups who could benefit from this message. In the era of the Million Man March on Washington, DC, the time was ripe for a celebration of the African American man in the arts, especially in terms of the rich, Gulf Coast musical tradition. Furthermore, I saw this project as an occasion for African American artists across generations and styles to talk to each other. I have always been impressed with the richness and variety of African American musical styles. Yet I have often been puzzled by the apparent lack of deference to the older generations and a lack of appreciation to the younger generations. Thus, my goal was to produce musical performances that would demonstrate these musical, historical, and cultural relationships. Blues musicians and rap performers in Houston are especially notorious for their intergenerational conflict. The following are typical charges: blues musicians often describe rappers as gangsters and troublemakers, whereas rappers sometimes see bluesmen as old "Toms" who perform old slave songs for the amusement of white audiences.

Subsequently, I designed and produced the "Black Men, Black Voices" project as a way of moving beyond simply talking, through media such as the formal interview, about the relationships among African American musicians across generations. I conceptualized "Black Men, Black Voices" as a type of synthetic performance ethnography (Kotarba 2004). This design has the producer creating the occasion for combined first- and second-order performance by assembling a cast of members/actors, and establishing the general topic for the performance, but allowing the members/actors to conduct their own conversations according to their interpretations of who they are, what their work is, and what they want to accomplish on stage. "Black Men, Black Voices" displays numerous cultural texts, which I will discuss later in conventional sociological terms (e.g., ethnicity, gender, and culture).

I produced six performances for the project in between 1998 and 2000. The first show was performed at the main auditorium at the Sunnyside Multi-Service Center on the far south side of Houston, to an audience ranging from pre-school children to the elderly. In the second show, a zydeco group from Louisiana performed on stage with a traditional Gulf Coast blues band, all in an intimate club in Houston before a Houston Blues Society audience. The third show was held at the University of Houston, Carl Lewis Auditorium, and consisted of four different bands (blues guitar band, blues keyboard band, zydeco, and spoken word/rap) taking turns playing and then chatting together about their different styles and traditions. The fourth program was a scripted performance at the Diverseworks Alternative Arts Space in Houston in 1998. Our performance was part of the "Ten Minute Max" series in which new or upcoming performers could present works lasting no more than ten minutes, to give the audience a taste of their creativity and vision. I produced a two-person act in which a young rapper, Kool B, and a veteran bluesman/guitar player, Texas Johnny Brown, took turns performing and commenting on each other's influence on them. Finally, we performed at a public high school and the 1998 Couch-Stone Symposium at the University of Houston.

The format for "Black Men, Black Voices" was informal and interactive. Someone hosted each performance, a job I have occasionally delegated to myself. I have also used the services of Houston Blues Society officers, such as Travis Peoples and Kathleen Kern, as hosts. The styles of

music represented include blues, jazz, gospel, rap, rhythm & blues, zydeco, and hip hop/spoken word. A total of twenty-six musicians participated in the performances. As the project developed, however, a core group
of musicians emerged. They were Pete Mayes (blues), Jackie Scott (gospel), and Kool B. These men had good chemistry working together, and
engaged in lively and insightful conversation on stage.

The Producer as Ethnographer

Performance ethnography is a fairly recent addition to interactional/
interpretive sociology. This activity originated in anthropology, communications, literature, the theater, and other disciplines in the 1980s in
which scholars attempted to expand the use of text—not data—as the
substance of culture most promising for analysis. Performance ethnography appeared in sociology in the 1990s as a strategy for addressing the
postmodernist "crisis in ethnography"—to borrow an anthropological
term (Marcus and Fischer 1986)—occurring in that discipline. In this brief
period, sociologists have constructed several styles of performance ethnography. Becker et al. (1989) created "performance science" by which
they transformed social scientific reports into dramatic scripts for dramatic readings. Richardson (e.g., 1994) has written and read numerous
poems, novels and short stories. Epstein (1997) produced a computer-
driven animation titled *Machine,* which dramatizes alienation and com-
modification in postmodern society.

The "Black Men, Black Voices" project differs from these earlier sociological performances because it does not use actors (sociologists or otherwise) to present second-order, fictionalized sociological accounts of
first-order, everyday life activities and events. On the contrary, "Black
Men, Black Voices" involves real people, each performing two related but
contrasting roles simultaneously. The first role enacted consists of the
musician's own personal biography, musical career, and personal
thoughts on music in general, the blues in particular, women, politics,
spirituality, and so forth. The second role is that of a generic, almost ideal
typical representative of all the male musicians in his category.

Thus, "Black Men, Black Voices" can thus be seen as a form of *natura-
listic performance* (Stucky 1993: 168–169). The role of the sociologist as
producer in "Black Men, Black Voices" is to create the circumstances and
possibility for the actors/artists/musicians to simply perform their music
by staging it. As several musicians in the project poignantly yet affection-
ately put it, I am the "ol' white guy who got the grant money." I exercised
very little control over the proceedings on stage once the performance
began, which is the way I wanted it to unfold. My only excursion into the
artistic delivery of "Black Men, Black Voices" was writing a list of suggested discussion questions for the host to direct to the musicians before
and after their musical performances. The musicians (and hosts, to a large

degree) took off on their own once the performance began. They shaped the performance according to their own musical values, expectations of what they believed I wanted them to do, and their own sense of what they wanted to accomplish on stage. The musicians often rejected my requests in favor of their own way of doing things. For example, the musicians almost all felt that their primary mission was to entertain the audience. They preferred to play their songs as if they were in a club or a recording studio, and let the audience "get out of it what they want," instead of engaging in any sort of analysis—which, of course, is my first reflex reaction as a sociologist. The music on the stage comprised a first-order musical performance in its own right. The musicians together created emergent scripts on stage that organized interaction related to their own music, interaction related to their musical style in general, and interaction related to their interpretation of the "Black Men, Black Voices" event itself.

To give the reader a feeling for the project I will provide a first-person account of the first performance of "Black Men, Black Voices." I wrote this account the day after the performance to capture the moment for future reading and analysis.

> Wow! I can't believe I got myself into this fix. Here I am, at the first performance of my "Black Men, Black Voices" project, and I don't have any Black men!! The main auditorium at the Sunnyside Multi-Service Center on the far south side of Houston is packed on this sunny Thursday morning. Alas, the only men in sight are several middle-age white guys from the local media, several students from my seminar in ethnographic methods, and me. Otherwise, I'm surrounded by approximately 100 senior citizens, 50 middle school kids, and about 35 preschoolers—all anxiously looking forward with great anticipation to this great display of African-American culture. Where is Jimmy Dotson, one of Houston's premier veteran bluesmen and guitar slingers; Kinney Abair, jazz guitarist and singer; Jackie Scott, gospel singer and pianist extraordinaire; and last, but not least, the Terrorists, a group of Fifth Ward rappers whose latest CD, "Full Scale Attack," is da bomb? . . .
>
> Well, everyone is here now except for the Terrorists. . . . Uh-oh, the Terrorists have arrived, ten of them walking slowly down the side isle to the stage. They're dressed in all-black baggies, with rags and caps, and of course dark sunglasses. The elderly women seem a bit perturbed if not scared; I should have told them ahead of time that the Terrorists prefer a dramatic entrance to their gigs.

Cultural Texts Displayed by "Black Men, Black Voices"

By observing the participants' (e.g., artists, audience, grantors, venue personnel, my colleagues at the university) performances from my privileged positions as producer and sociologist, I was able to see numerous sociological themes in the proceedings. The following is a partial list of the most important of these themes. Let us return to the Sunnyside Multi-Service Center for starters.

"Black Men, Black Voices" displayed ethnic texts. As producer, I felt considerable pressure to make sure the project met fairly high artistic (read: Anglo, middle-age, and middle-class) standards. Colleagues on the Board of Directors of the Houston Blues Society, colleagues at the university, staff members at the various granting agencies, and others all felt my project could and should be very elegant and worthy of comparison with (what they thought were) similar projects involving folk singer-songwriters, poets, mystery writers, and so forth. Some of those in attendance at Sunnyside were appalled that my artists were not on time and ready to perform on schedule. As a sociologist however, I interpreted artists' demeanor—as well as all other activities in the project—as normal. Blues and jazz musicians do not routinely perform at 9 a.m. when the rest of us are already caffeined out. When Jimmy Dotson and Kinney Abair finally arrived, they proceeded to "play the dozens" on stage in front of the largely African-American audience. The topic was paternity. Kinney kept referring to Jimmy as an old man (both are in their sixties), whereas Jimmy kept referring to himself as Kinney's daddy who was going to teach him a thing or two about playing the guitar. The African Americans in the audience loved the teasing and the one-upmanship; some Anglo members of the audience were critical of the "lack of professionalism."

"Black Men, Black Voices" displayed generational texts. When the Terrorists finally arrived, they freaked everyone out, with the possible exception of the middle school kids. The entered the auditorium en masse. There were nine young African American men dressed like gangsters, with dark sunglasses, gold chains, wide-legged baggy pants, and combat boots. Bless their hearts, the senior citizens thought for a moment that we were being held up by a bunch of local neighborhood thugs! Again, I treated the event as normal. Rap artists routinely travel in entourage with their "associates," which according to insiders is a social structure borrowed from gang culture. Everyone settled down when the Terrorists climbed up on the stage and took their place next to Jimmy and Kinney. The middle school kids immediately tuned into the Terrorists' accounts of everyday life and growing up in Houston's impoverished Fifth Ward. Many of the elderly audience members apparently did, too.

"Black Men, Black Voices" displayed social class texts. As I indicated above, Kathleen Kern, a Houston Blues Society officer and local radio personality, served as host for one of our performances. Kathleen is quite a character. She is a reforming hippie from my generation who, like many baby boomers, turned to the blues as a way of keeping the music and experiences of the 1960s in their lives. She is originally from Georgia and has maintained her thick Georgia accent. She is self-defined as "white trash," an identity that causes no problem for her many African

American friends, fans, and admirers, but freaks out many middle-class Anglos in the crowd.

For example, our performance at the Mucky Duck, a classy little folk music club in Houston, attracted many university types (read: Anglo, middle class, and culturally imposing). This is the crowd that prefers to talk about blues music in condescending and boring terms such as "indigenous" or "folk music." Several of these people were appalled at Kathleen's demeanor, her thick southern accent, and her way of talking to the musicians (e.g., calling them "baby" and referring to the young musicians on stage as "young studs"). When I raised this issue to the musicians after the show, they seemed more disturbed by the white audience member who called out for them to cover a popular B.B. King song they detested. To them, Kathleen was what she was supposed to be . . . white trash. They felt comfortable with the long-standing, accommodating relationship between working-class Anglos and African Americans in the local blues music scene. They loved her. No problem.

"Black Men, Black Voices" displayed gendering texts. The observation is commonly made that women in blues do not receive either the recognition, acclaim or the paying gigs that the men receive. Further, recent music criticism argues that male-dominated blues over the years has generally portrayed women in demeaning if not pornographic ways (e.g., Lomax 1993: 379). The "Black Men, Black Voices" project created the occasion for the display of the everyday life texts by which gender issues are negotiated and acted out in the blues scene. We observed how the scene contained both traditional male-centered and feminist texts. Although the focus of the project was on men, I soon heard many calls for establishing a similar project involving blues women. The "Black Men, Black Voices" project in fact created the opportunity for a subsequent "Blues-N-Kids" project on women musicians by highlighting the centrality of gender in the blues.

A more immediate effect of the "Black Men, Black Voices" project was the discussion during performances of the various ways different styles of music portray women. I introduced this topic as producer, again at the urging of several female members of the Houston Blues Society, when I constructed a list of suggested topics for discussion. The musicians accounted for gender in their work the following (paraphrased) ways. The bluesmen and rappers both argued that the portrayal of women in their blues lyrics may appear sexist to middle-class, Anglo audiences, when it is in fact a factual reflection of the style of interaction between African American men and women. Further, to call these lyrics "pornographic" is to demean the healthy celebration of sexuality in an African American community traditionally denied other forms of pleasure because of racism. The gospel musicians noted that the style of their music per se prohibited sexual content, and that the portrayal of believers and sinners is generally not differentiated by gender. The jazz and zydeco musicians noted that their styles generally portray women in romantic terms. The hip hop/spoken word artists displayed the feminist turn in their work through their readings of African American women as partners in the black experience, heroines in the struggle against oppression, people worthy of respect, and even co-performers at times.

Enjoying the Role of the Baby Boomer Producer

As Johannes Fabian (1990) argues, "Ethnography is essentially, not incidentally, communicative or dialogical; conversation, not observation, should be the key to conceptualizing ethnographic knowledge production" (17). The "Black Men, Black Voices" project produced conversations among different generations and styles of African American musicians, audience members, funding agency officials, critics, and so forth.

I experienced the role of the producer in ways totally compatible with intellectual and literary accounts of life in a postmodern cultural world (e.g., Kroker 1993). At times I felt I was almost tripping on the fluidity of identities I acquired and projected. I felt like a producer when I wrote grant proposals, managed the budget, booked the talent, contracted with vendors and club owners, and wrote and disseminated press releases. I felt like one of the talent when I realized I had to develop an acceptable and competent style of presentation of self when I introduced the artists on stage. I felt like a designer when I designed the graphics for fliers and posters. I felt like a director when I helped shape the course of a performance through suggested topics of discussion. I felt like a critic when I conversed with the musicians about audience expectations and commented to them on completed performances. Some of my most pleasurable moments, however, occurred when I felt like a member of the audience, simply enjoying the work of these fine musicians.

Yet there were moments when I felt like a stranger to my own creation, which was good. I viewed a performance as a sociologist from an analytical distance—seeing those invisible sociological things no one else present could see. As a sociologist, I was also in the enviable position of being able to ignore if not waive the conventional values by which art is evaluated (cf. Lyotard 1984). Thus, when my musicians were late or when a guitar was out of tune, I sought and analyzed others' reactions to these events. Put differently, participants in "Black Men, Black Voices" could do nothing wrong when I viewed events as a sociologist. I was in the enviable position of enjoying mistakes, omissions, and lapses, and framing them as normal conditions of normal social interaction.

The issue of aesthetics remains to be addressed, that is how to assess the value of the "Black Men, Black Voices" artistic performances (cf. Jameson 1983). Value equates with beauty in the arts, and consists of the pleasures a performance brings to the audience, the critics, and so on. To keep things real (that is, natural), I left the aesthetics work to the audience, including my sociological colleagues. A common response from my colleagues who attended several performances was their pleasure at seeing just how poetic and constructive rap music could be, based on Al "Kool B" Le Blanc's (1998) elegant reading of original rap poetry. One well-received piece is "Coke Adds Life":

> It ain't no pretty poetry thing
> When urban school bells riiiiiiing, and
> Little ones,
> Would be soldiers
> Fall lame to the claim that coke adds life.

In terms of lay experiences, a pleasure for lay audience members is to hear talk about the historical context of the evolution of African American music. Although sociologists vary greatly in their emphasis on the importance of history for sociological analysis, the audience sees history as an indication that the performance is serious, scholarly, important, and worth experiencing since it is very different from their own, everyday experiences of popular music. The producer's responsibility, though, is to make it clear to the audience that the ethnographic interpretation of African American music is in no way superior to lay interpretations.

As I mentioned earlier, performance ethnography has become very popular among baby boomer interactionists. In order for a sociologist to stay actively engaged in his or her work, it has had to be important, stimulating, constructive, and positively reviewed by our various audiences. Now, it is also possible for sociology to be *fun*. The essential pleasure of "Black Men, Black Voices," to anyone fortunate to be in the audience, lies in its great success as music. To see and hear Jackie Scott take a traditional blues song and play both its blues and gospel versions on the keyboard brings chills to all present, and got even the most atheistic social scientists in the crowd hand clapping. To witness a senior bluesman like Pete Mayes and a young hip hop artist like "Kool B" talk about the neglected (by white critics) spiritual dimensions of their music on Juneteenth Day (Emancipation Day in Texas) was an experience I could never get from more conventional ethnographic strategies, let alone textbooks on race and ethnicity. The pleasure derived from the music or art is a necessary if not sufficient standard by which we should evaluate performance ethnography.

EIGHT

The Timekeeper Self

Most sociologists include at least an implicit sense of time in their writing.[9] As Reese and Katovich (1989) note, sociologists have approached the study of time both structurally and interactionally. Structurally, the focus is on time as observable yet typically taken-for-granted features of social life, or "temporal structure." Temporal structures organize social life for us, while it is our responsibility as competent members of society to abide by normatively approved time markers. Interactionally, time is viewed as an integral tool in everyday life (Couch 1985; Mead 1934). We use time—time frames, timing, and timeliness—to make sense of situations, events, and relationships. We use time to make sense of the world and to create social order, for as Reese and Katovich (1989: 161) state, "Of fundamental importance to interactionism is the production of action timed with the reciprocal acts of others so that social alignments can be achieved."

Symbolic interactionists have studied time in three general ways. First, there are fairly general theories of time, such as Flaherty's (1999) discussion of the experience of time. Second, there are analyses of time-specific phenomena, such as Snow and Brissett's (1986) essay on pauses and Maines's (1983) work on the life course. Third, interactionists have used notions of time as analytical tools to help them better understand other social phenomena, such as Reese and Katovich's (1989) analysis of deviance and Denzin's (1987) analysis of alcoholism.

In this chapter, I take the third interactionist approach insofar as I will use the notion of time to help me understand baby boomers' experiences of rock 'n' roll (Kotarba 2002c). *Time* serves as a sensitizing concept in this analysis (Blumer 1954). A sensitizing concept is an idea that serves to direct research, raise certain research questions, and allow if not encourage the researcher to begin analyzing the social phenomenon in question.

My awareness of the sensitizing concept of time has helped me discover and make sense of interesting aspects of baby boomers' experiences of rock 'n' roll that the researcher and actor might ordinarily take for granted. I will describe the ways this cohort uses time to organize their lives with music and to organize their music with life events. I will follow Flaherty's (1999: 4–5) search for the ways self, situation and time interact.

TEMPORAL STRUCTURES IN THE WORLD OF ROCK 'N' ROLL

Songs are the temporal structures that comprise the actual stuff of the world of rock 'n' roll. There have been literally dozens of popular songs written and performed with the word "time" in them. A few frequently mentioned by respondents in my work include "By the Time I Get to Phoenix" by Glen Campbell in 1968, "Time" by the Chambers Brothers in 1969, and "Time (Is on My Side)" by the Rolling Stones in 1970. Interestingly, I did not find any respondents who organized their personal tastes in or experiences with music in terms of songs about time. When questioned, they readily offered categories such as songs about love, war/peace, fun, cars, drugs, and other substantive topics.

Some respondents have been involved at various times in the music industry, occupying such roles as artist, producer, roadie, sound person, and DJ. The work of creating and performing music is structured by time as much as in any other social organizational activity (cf. Zerubavel's [1979] study of time patterns in the modern hospital). Significant issues involving time include the tight scheduling of recording time in the studio; the tour stop calendar; scheduling record release dates to coincide with the holiday gift buying season, making the most of one's musical career while one still has time before the fifteen minutes of celebrity evaporate; and so forth.

"NOSTALGIA ISN'T WHAT IT USED TO BE": DECADE VERSUS COHORT ANALYSIS

Musical nostalgia is important to my research because it occasions the intersection of structural and interactional versions of time. Structurally, journalists and other mass media workers have popularized the idea of the "decade" by using it as a simple and convenient framework for portraying history in a nostalgic framework. This framework provides the opportunity to collect and arrange events to create new copy and special magazine issues. For example, the November 1990 issue of *Rolling Stone* magazine is presented as "A Special Issue: The 80s." This social construction of a ten-year period includes the following articles: "Bruce Springsteen: His Was the Voice of the Eighties—But What Was He Really Saying?"; "Madonna: Hers Was the Image of the 80s—Vamp, Tramp, Star,

Madonna"; and so forth. *Rolling Stone* has assembled similar special issues for the 1960s, 1990s, and 2000s.

The journalistic use of the "decade" has become a taken-for-granted
feature of our public culture. Common associations between decades and
music include the Roaring Twenties and the Charleston; the 1940s and
big band dance music; the 1950s and early rock 'n' roll music; the 1960s
and the Beatles; the 1970s and disco music; the 1990s and rap music; and
the 2000s as the return of pop. Accordingly, decade-based nostalgia
serves as a valuable marketing tool. The specific products are numerous:
oldies radio stations, 1950s hamburgers and shakes diners with jukebox-
es, Beatles compilation CD box sets for holiday giving, and so forth.

Numerous music scholars have critiqued the popular use of the *decade*
to create a popular history. Todd Gitlin (1987) is one of many observers
who decry the idea fostered by the mass media that the 1960s were somehow a unified period of countercultural activism. Although the 1960s
have been perhaps the single most heralded, analyzed, and written about
decade, it also marks a period in rock 'n' roll music most notably marked
by diversity . . . from the Beach Boys and rhythm and blues to the Grateful Dead and Led Zeppelin.

Symbolic interactionist views on nostalgia focus on the cognitive and
interactional tools members use to organize past experience and the feelings associated with it. Davis (1979) has written one of the most comprehensive interactionist theories of nostalgia. He argues that nostalgic
thoughts and talks about the past are, by definition, "always infused with
imputations of past beauty, pleasure, joy, satisfaction, goodness, happi-
ness, love, and the like, in sum, any or several of the positive affects of
being" (Davis 1979: 14). Nostalgic experiences help the individual maintain the sense of continuity in self-identity always threatened by changes
occasioned by life-cycle events (Davis 1979: 52). In his search for mecha-
nisms people actually use in everyday life to categorize experiences of the
past, Davis downplays the importance of the mass media driven,
decades-based nostalgia in favor of the idea of the *generation*. For example, people are more likely to individually and collectively coalesce
around specific historical events than "simple chronological references
(like decades) per se" (Davis 1979: 113). We would therefore expect gen-
eration-driven categories like Generation X and the Baby Boomer Generation to resonate well with many people.

My research on baby boomer rock 'n' roll fans suggests the value of
expanding Davis's ideas on generations to the more general concept of
cohort. Very few respondents used notions of decade in interview to identify themselves or conceptualize past experiences. In fact, a more typical
response was to distance oneself from the embarrassment of identifying
or being identified with overly commercialized decade talk. Francine is a
sixty-one-year-old accountant, wife, and mother of three who commented on the stereotypical 1950s musical produced at Disney World: "We

took the kids to see the show. It was a lot of fun for them, the leather jackets and greasy hair. . . . No, I told them their father and I never dressed like that. God knows we weren't greasers."

Bob is a fifty-eight-year-old civil engineer whom I interviewed on the lawn of a summer Styx and Kansas concert at the Mitchell Pavilion in Houston. His date for the concert was his wife of thirty-three years, who listened to these bands with Bob when they were college students at "Midwestern University:"

> The '60s? Was I there? [Laugh] You know, the music they [music writ-ers] say we listened to in the '60s, stuff like the Stones and the British Blues bands, hell, we didn't get into them until after college. We wer-en't all hippies, you know, you should remember that. We drank and did the Beach Boys most of the time.

I have found that my respondents use numerous cohort configurations of their own device with which to identify and to make sense of the past. Let me briefly discuss two: the *class cohort* and the *musical style*. The class cohort ordinarily refers to graduating classes, whether from elementary, middle, or high school, or college. A common practice that can be traced at least as far back as the baby boomer generation's school days is for a class to choose its own song—informally, by vote, or by class officers—as a collective logo. These songs are played or performed at senior proms and graduation parties. They can be heard at class reunions many years later. Popular class songs for baby boomers include—among many oth-ers—Chubby Checker's "The Twist" (1960) ; Sheb Wooley's " Purple Peo-ple Eater" (1961); the Beatles' "Yesterday" (1967); Dion's "Abraham, Mar-tin and John" (1969); and Led Zeppelin's "Stairway to Heaven" (1971).

The musical style is a very common and meaningful mechanism for the management of everyday life and the past. Musical styles are espe-cially relevant to baby boomers because the intricate differentiation of musical styles began during their youth in the 1960s and 1970s. It was not simply rock 'n' roll anymore—there were dance songs, car songs, drug songs, and so on. Invoking a musical style also eliminates the need to know actual dates, years, and other precise time markers implicit in the idea of a decade. For example, Ray is a fifty-eight-year-old army sergeant who recalled the relationship between southern rock and life as a teenag-er:

> When I was in high school, all we listened to was redneck rockers, you know, ZZ Top, Allman Brothers, Lynyrd Skynyrd. They sounded just great driving around (small town, Texas) after football games.

Respondents talk about treating musical styles as if they were posses-sions. You can take them with you over the years like old friends (e.g., Bob Dylan); discard them when identification with them is no longer fashionable (e.g., heavy metal); or acquire new ones to fit emerging identities (e.g., new age).

THE REFLEXIVE RELATIONSHIP BETWEEN ROCK 'N' ROLL AND TIME IN MIDDLE AGE

According to Henri Bergson (1922: 44), time is one of the fundamental primordial experiences. We are inherently aware of our temporality, that is, the perception that our lives have pasts, presents, and futures. We are self-conscious of our location in duration, but sociologically, understand that we learned self-consciousness through interaction with others (Mead 1934). For baby boomers, duration has been going on for some years, and time is experienced in terms of one's awareness of the existential and social implications of getting old.

Music is a cultural resource that helps to meaningfully locate the self in extended duration. For example, several respondents noted that the recent deaths of baby boomer generation artists—such as Davy Jones, Levon Helm, Robin Gibbs, and Gil Scott-Heron cannot be ignored or denied because these afflictions may be more the result of aging than the excessive lifestyles associated with the premature deaths of artists such as Janice Joplin, Jim Morrison, and Whitney Houston. Regardless of the baby boomer fan's past or current lifestyles, the toll of aging is universal.

Middle-age rock 'n' rollers are also more conscious of the significance of personal events such as anniversaries. Music is a convenient medium for gift-giving, for example, in the form of boxed CD sets containing the couple's "our song" in a digitalized version. Anniversary parties are commonly conducted to a soundtrack of music popular at the time the couple was dating.

REVISITING BABY BOOMERS AND TIME

The ideas presented in this chapter only touch on the many and varied ways time appears as a feature in the everyday life of baby boomer rock 'n' roll fans. As one would expect, there are important gender, ethnicity, and social class factors not discussed here. There are numerous other ways of sociological significance that time enters people's lives that I can only mention here, but I explore in the broader study. For example, baby boomers were the first generation who grew up with a music-based mechanism demarcating the "week" as a crucial timeframe for youth: the radio "Top 40" list issued at the local record store every Friday afternoon (see also Rothenbuhler 1985). As baby boomers get older, they find themselves increasingly "passing time" as the aging process dictates. I found myself in the hospital several years ago undergoing and recovering from the bane of middle age: colon surgery. My loving wife visited me often, not really to do much except to spend time with me . . . to "sit with me" as my mother would say. How did we spend one particular Friday evening in St. Luke's? Naturally, we watched the Sting special on the A&E channel—discussing how well Sting has aged; how nice his short-cropped hair style goes with his thinning hair; dissing the Land Rover commercials geared toward baby boomers with lots of money to spend on gas (with obviously no children in college!), and quietly enjoying the fact that we both like Sting and his hip-yet-mellow soft rock music.

In conclusion, the essential point in this chapter as in all interactionist research on time, is the one made by George Herbert Mead in *The Philosophy of the Act* over sixty years ago: "A past was never in the form in which it appears as a past. Its reality is in its interpretation of the present" (1938: 616). Symbolic interaction is a marvelous strategy for studying the everyday life of a generational cohort like baby boomer rock 'n' roll fans because it treats the individual as an agent who actively conducts the interactional work of the present.

NINE

Adult Pop/Rock Music Scenes: A Global Survey

As we have seen in chapter 7, blues music and culture provide an accommodating home for the baby boomer seeking friendly and comfortable — yet public and social — musical experiences. The blues is only one example of the more general concept of *music scene*. This concept provides us a very useful tool for understanding the comprehensive social worlds in which various participants — those who create music as well as those who appreciate music — work hard to produce a magnificent alternative reality that lies at the essence of the baby boomer experience. The concept also fits well with understanding musical experiences in other cultures and societies.

THE SOCIAL SCENE

Any social scene is primarily an ideational entity; scenes are not real places. Scenes exist in our minds and become visible during interaction. Social scenes are ideas that are larger and more socially powerful than their individual components. Social scenes are in fact greater than the sum of their parts. Nevertheless, I will itemize and discuss the key components of music scenes — but first, I will briefly examine the key theoretical statements on social scenes in the sociological literature.

SOCIOLOGICAL WRITINGS ON THE MUSIC SCENE

John Irwin published a very influential book in 1977 titled, simply, *Scenes*. Irwin taught sociology at San Francisco State University, and was a notable criminologist. As a resident of San Francisco during the culturally and politically turbulent 1960s and 1970s, Irwin was struck by the creative evolution of public life, especially entertainment activities in a city that has given us the Beat Generation, Haight-Ashbury, and the Grateful Dead. Entertainment in San Francisco seemed to be organized by streets and neighborhoods, in terms sometimes referred to by urban sociologists as *subcultures*. The concept of the subculture, though, implies hidden if not deviant social life, and Irwin wisely chose not to restrict his viewpoint on scenes that way. Scenes, in other words, provide occasions to celebrate the wonder of living in the modern city.

The scene is an inclusive concept that involves everyone related to a cultural phenomenon, such as artists, audiences, management, vendors, and critics. The ecological location of the phenomenon is also critical because it provides a sense of place and predictability to a scene, in such commonsense terms as districts, clubs, recording studios, and rehearsal rooms. The products of this interaction, for example, ads, concerts, recordings, and critical reviews, give meaning to the scene.

Irwin focused on entertainment-oriented phenomena, such as music, theater, and dance, in his book. Participation in these kinds of scenes is expressive and offers direct gratification, not future gratification. One ordinarily goes to a music club to enjoy the music, have a few drinks, meet new or old friends, dance, and do other things that involve immediate please or reward. John Irwin would not consider my undergraduate course in "The Sociology of Popular Music" a music scene because the primary purpose of participating in the course is future-oriented: completing a course for academic credit toward a university degree. (I will not even suggest that my course meets the "fun" quotient expected when participating in a true music scene!)

Given the cultural flux that was pervasive in San Francisco at the time, John Irwin was especially fascinated by emerging (or new) scenes. Both gay bars in the Castro District and fern bars in respectable, middle-class neighborhoods, for example, were characterized by "less tightly written" scripts so that "the actors are freer to engage in somewhat spontaneous acting with others in particular social settings" (Irwin 1977: 194). Social scenes crave originality and creativity—in dress, demeanor, and ways of talking.

Finally, social scenes are places where the participants are expected to remain open to interaction with others. That is part of the deal when spending time in a scene. When one is sitting at the bar in a music club, one is susceptible to being approached by others. Whether one is asked to dance, have a drink, or talk, one is expected to reply in a meaningful if not polite way, unlike the response called for when approached by a stranger on a dark street. Again, John Irwin argues clearly that a scene like the Castro is not merely a collection of bars or businesses: it is an attitude, a sense of anticipation, a source of excitement, and perhaps even a home. The Castro is greater than the sum of its parts. Although Irwin focused his analysis on scenes catering primarily to young people (e.g., drinking and surfing), there is no reason his concept cannot be applied to entertainment experiences of older participants, such as middle-age and older rock 'n' roll fans.

Andy Bennett and Richard A. Peterson (2004) wrote specifically about music scenes, especially emergent scenes catering to young audiences. They see three types of music scenes.

Local music scenes are those confined to specific areas. Examples include the south side Chicago blues scene, and local rave scenes. Another example would be Sixth Street in Austin, Texas (cf. Shank 1994). Local scenes are geographically and historically unique. To some degree, and at least until they gain fame or notoriety, a local scene can be self-supporting and exclusive. Everyone wanted or needed for a scene to exist or be vibrant can be located there.

Translocal music scenes involve the coming together of scattered local scenes. The Vans Warped Tour and regional or national music festivals are examples of scenes that are united as communicative, informational, and aesthetic networks. Translocal scenes can be thought of as situational. Participants may communicate via the Internet or even analog newsletters, but will generally emerge in physical settings on a regular basis. The South-by-Southwest music festival (SXSW), held every March in Austin, Texas, is supported by a constant Internet presence during the remaining months of the year. In chapter 11 of this book, we will see how Americana is one of the fastest growing translocal scenes for baby boomer rock 'n' rollers.

Virtual music scenes are scenes that exist completely online but, more specifically, do not need analog activities or settings for their vitality let alone survival. Bennett and Peterson (2004) cite alternative country, post rock, and Kate Bush as virtual scenes that support their analog parallels. We need only look at the numerous listservs and Twitter sites (e.g., www.dead.net) dedicated to the Grateful Dead to find virtual music scenes populated by baby boomers that are self-sufficient and thriving. It is somewhat obvious that aging baby boomers would find increasing difficulty getting out to attend various concerts performed by Grateful Dead reunion and tribute bands. One of the silliest phenomena I have observed in writing this book is the aging Deadhead hanging around some concert related to the Dead, such as the annual Willie Nelson Fourth of July Picnic in Texas, wearing a Dead shirt from the distant past, much too small and short for his or her aging—and evolving, to be kind—stomach.

THE SELF AND PLACE

One of the most important ways that people utilize the music scene is to assist in the process of the becoming of self. As noted earlier, existential social thought reminds us that the self is continuously evolving, changing, and adapting in and to a useful, meaningfully rich, and consensual sense of place is the desirable outcome of participation in music scenes. We engage in a reflexive relationship with the places we occupy. We make places as places make us, our selves, and our identities (Gruenewald 2003: 621). Sara Cohen (1995: 434) has stated that "music plays a role in producing place as a material setting compromising the physical and built environment; as a setting for everyday social relations, practices and interactions; and as a concept or symbol that is represented or interpreted." The consumption and production of music also draw people together and symbolize their sense of collectivity and place.

For baby boomers, place has two primary meanings. The first is the meaning for the location of the scene where the music is performed and enjoyed. Bobby, a sixty-five-year-old city worker, sees the Mitchell Pavilion in the Woodlands, Texas—just north of Houston—as a sacred location:

> This is where I first saw the Rolling Stones play. It was in 1966, I believe. Man, what a trip! We sat up on the hill, no blankets, no nothing . . . The place was like magic. It was unusually cool and breezy. You could just lay back and watch the stars as Mick [Jagger] acted the fool. You know, you would always go to concerts back then to meet chicks. That night with the Stones—you just needed to be there.

The second meaning for place is the symbolic place created by the musical experience. Music can transport the self to places far beyond the physical location where the music is actually experienced. Music can also create places where the participant can find solace and security of self.

To further explore the dynamics of place in baby boomers' music, I will turn to the significance of place in three global music scenes: Latino music scenes, Polish music scenes, and music scenes associated with the political uprisings and resistance movements in North Africa and the Middle East. The analysis for Latino music scenes is derived from an extensive, two-year, team field research project I organized with a group of sociology graduate students at the University of Houston (Kotarba et al. 2009; Nowotny et al. 2010).[10] We examined a wide range of Latino music scenes in the Houston metropolitan area, including emerging scenes such as rock en Espanol, gay Latino dance music, professional soccer supporters' music, and religious music (Kotarba et al. 2009). For our discussion here, I will examine three styles of Latino music that are largely performed by adult artists, and that attract and are utilized by a predominantly adult audience: conjunto, mariachi, and salsa. The analysis for Polish music scenes is derived from ongoing research conducted in Poland and Houston with adult Polish citizens and Polish Americans (Kotarba 2002b). The analysis of *hybrid* rap music scenes in North Africa and the Middle East are derived from an ongoing Internet study of these quickly evolving events (Kotarba and LaLone 2011).

THE VARIETIES OF LATINO MUSIC SCENES

In a large, southwestern city like Houston, there are numerous styles of Latino music and, subsequently, numerous music scenes. In designing our team study of Latino music, I divided them into two types: *emerging* and *established* music scenes. There were two essential reasons for doing this. First, Houston has been home to various Latino communities over many decades. Although not exclusive to them, the established music scenes are largely associated with long-term residents and their communities. Second, the established music scenes are also associated with older Latinos/as, the focus of the present book. The reader should keep in mind that Latino/a baby boomers do take part in the more recent, emerging Latino music scenes, but are not the driving force behind their success or their musical styles.

In the broader study from which the present analysis is derived, we investigated a number of features of music scenes in order to assemble a comprehensive portrait of music in the Latino community (e.g., artists, audiences, and the music) (Kotarba et al. 2009; Nowotny et al. 2010). For our purposes here, I will focus on the role adults—especially as parents—play in those scenes. I will also focus on the sense of place intended and created by Latino music scenes.

The Conjunto Scene

The roots of conjunto music are firmly embedded in the traditional culture and values of northern Mexico and Texas. Emerging in the early 1900s, the lyrics, instrumentation, and melody artfully recreate the traditional Mexican folk music of ranchera (traditional Mexican music performed with voice and guitar and bolero (slow tempo dance music) of that time period (Guerra 2001). The notions of family and traditional cultural values play a key role in the continued popularity of conjunto music, specifically in the Houston area. According to Valdez and Halley (1996) conjunto is a "durable and significant cultural expression among working-class and poor Mexican Americans. It has also served as a cultural vehicle for reproducing gender roles in more traditional forms that are typical of the majority society." Tejano music, which is very similar to conjunto, is flourishing in the Houston area. Though similar in style and content (both feature the accordion), Tejano music blends Texas and

American country, western, and rock n' roll with the traditional *conjunto* sound. Often referred to as *Norteño* (i.e., of the North), Tejano music is best described as the music of Texas Mexicans and an emerging music scene especially popular with young people (Kotarba et al. 2009).

Conjunto utilizes the unique sound of the accordion accompanied by a German polka-style beat, traditional instrumentation, and arrangements. An important facet of Texas-Mexican music is the exclusive use of the diatonic accordion, that is, an accordion that utilizes one, two, or three rows of buttons (instead of piano keys) to differentiate notes. This traditional type of accordion differs from the "piano accordions" used in Cajun, rockabilly, and even modern Norteño music (Nowotny et al. 2010: 33).

The sound of a true conjunto ensemble is designed to showcase the accordionist. Drums and electric bass provide traditional rhythms and help keep the beat, as in any pop/rock band. Unlike modern rock, however, which is characterized by boisterous guitar leads, conjunto employs the banjo sexto as another rhythm instrument. The addition of lyrics is recent to conjunto. Incorporating the singing tradition of the guitarreros (guitarists) into their music, pioneer accordionists began to add song lyrics with duet harmonies to their instrumental dance music (Peña 1985).

The role of lyrics is constantly discussed in Houston's conjunto music scene. Traditional conjunto, which was performed only for dance, does not have lyrics or vocal melodies; purists prefer an instrumental ensemble. The musicians who play this pure form of *conjunto* create a joyously nostalgic mood that senior audience members relish. One male performer particularly enjoyed putting his own interpretation on the music, commenting: "If I'm happy, it keeps me happy, and if I'm sad it makes me happy." When lyrics are incorporated into *conjunto* music, romanticized depictions of lost or unrequited love are the most popular subjects. A female musician described the songs: "I like the fact that live conjunto music is not just a show but a form of expression. The songs are associated with real life experiences such as heartbreak, prison time, or working at the job and this is sincere and more genuine when it is heard live" (Nowotny et al. 2010: 35).

The lyrics express emotions that respondents feel cannot be expressed accurately outside of the original Spanish language. Many conjunto artists are sensitive to the unique demands of their multilingual audience, and they utilize a combination of Spanish and English lyrics, while trying to stay true to the original conception of the song. The vocalist and accordionist for a popular local band discusses the compromise necessary to appeal to both audiences:

> I think that mixing lyrics in Spanish and English makes a more interesting blend. Even when every listener doesn't understand what is being

said, the music speaks for itself, and it seems like someone is actually translating the words for you. (Nowotny et al. 2010: 34)

For this artist, maintaining authenticity is not typically as relevant as pleasing the audience (Kotarba 2009).

Sense of place. The audience for conjunto music consists of predominantly second or third generation Mexican Americans. They often refer to themselves as Tejanos, like the robust Mexican citizens who inhabited the Texas Frontier in the eighteenth and nineteenth centuries. A common theme among fans of this scene is a strong sense of nostalgia and historical appreciation of the music and its characters. When Albert listens to live *conjunto* he says, "I feel like I am at home. I feel like I have something in common with other people and a sense of camaraderie fills my heart." Because the music is often enjoyed at family gatherings and traditional celebrations, there is an inherently conservative connection between conjunto and the past. Reynosa eloquently described this conservative connection when he explained his motivations for playing conjunto:

We don't have a master plan, we just want to go out there and entertain our fans and have a good time. We're all good friends and enjoying this opportunity. Every time we perform, I know this is going to bring back a lot of great memories for the fans and for everyone involved.

Louis described how he enjoyed "the music I grew up on." Maria noted, "This is my grandparents' music and I want my grandchildren to love it too." Roberto described the connection among the different generations in his family in detail:

I listen [to *conjunto*] because I grew up with it and it's traditional music that I can hold long conversations about the artists with my dad and grandfather . . . it bridges the gap of generations where you look forward to spending time with your parents and grandparents simply because you love the same kind of music. I think others listen to it for almost the same reasons . . . others would probably say it's great music to dance to—once you get the beat, you can't help but move. (Nowotny et al. 2010: 35)

Traditional conjuntos were actually written and performed for family gatherings. Groups were (and still are) often comprised of relatives who perform together at birthdays, holidays, and *quinceañeras* (birthday party for fifteen year old females). As one respondent noted, "[Listening to conjunto] reminds me of family gatherings at my grandparents' house . . . surrounded by good music, friends . . . reminds me of home." Using a shared knowledge of traditional songs and dances, families are able to celebrate together, each finding something in conjunto to fit their musical tastes (Nowotny et al. 2010: 35).

Modern conjunto is still a family experience. Traditional songs and dances are passed on from generation to generation. One respondent felt it was particularly important to expose his young son to the music, stating, "I want to teach him to be aware of our culture. And now at this stage in my life, I find myself having to tell him of what this unique area had, how it evolved and what it became, because we had to create our own identity through our music." He also spoke at length concerning regional identity, and how he wanted his son to understand the unique situation that faced early Tejanos, particularly the ambiguous nature of identifying as a Tejano people that were "accepted neither by the Mexicanos on the other side of the border nor by the Anglos on this side." Likewise, Sam enjoys conjunto because he sees it as part of his cultural tradition, "I truly enjoy [conjunto], the beats the rhythms . . . I like the way it makes me feel—it gives me a sense of family and home. I don't like the way it's shunned by most . . . this music represents our roots—the heart of our culture."

Because the music is written to accompany dances, several respondents likened their love of conjunto to their love of dance. Conjunto's blend of polka, waltz, and western swing appeals to those who favor traditional European and American dance styles. According to one musician,

> The benefits (of listening to *conjunto*) to me are purely cultural. The *conjunto* music is music that was started by common people in Texas but with major influences from other (ethnic groups), such as the Germans, Czechs, and Russians. Because it is common in many cultures I think that people listen to it.

There is a strong identification among audience members to life's seemingly universal dilemmas (relationship issues, longing, and loss) coupled with conjunto promise of dancing one's cares away. Luis illustrated this point when he said,

> Once the music starts it grabs you and doesn't let go . . . it takes you for a ride, from fast pace to [a] slow couple [of] songs to songs that make you move your hips like the *cumbias* . . .I guess in one word—Cantina music (bar music)—everybody is out to have a great time with family and friends . . . [*Conjuntos*] play anywhere from the backyard at a birthday party to family weddings to local clubs, to all over Texas even to out of state fairs, even other countries like Japan! . . . The crowd that attends *conjunto* events is there for fun and the music just brings out good times in you!" (Nowotny et al. 2010: 36)

Conjunto is the music of the past. It is interpreted in modern forms (i.e., Tejano and norteno), but it is steeped in tradition. Fans of the conjunto scene in Houston enjoy the music because it gives them a direct connection to their past. By listening to same music as their ancestors, they are able to share in a tradition that predates even the state of Texas. Therefore, the resultant sense of place is matched by a sense of time. Whether they are reminded of a time and place they have only heard about, or they remember their grandparents introducing them to the music and dance of South Texas, conjunto consistently transports its listeners to an earlier time and place. Additionally, conjunto music tied to a very real sense of place—the actual physical, geographic location of Southern Texas and Northern Mexico.

I will reiterate the pervasive theme in our conversations with musicians and audience members, that is, the importance of passing the conjunto musical traditions on to one's children. As is the case with most ethnic groups I have encountered in my research, music serves as a primary instrument for socializing children to one's ethnic identity. Dance, of course, is a closely related instrument.

Latino Music: Mariachi

The mariachi tradition emerged in the post-revolutionary period of the 1920s as a symbol of Mexican identity (Jaquez 2002). The charro suit in which mariachis perform is an important national symbol for Mexico and the suit symbolizes manhood, nationhood, and power (Vanderwood 1981).

In the Houston area, the mariachi scene can be found in two distinct locations: in public locations such as Mexican restaurants and concerts; and at private family and community events. The reader may have seen and heard them perform *al talon*, for a fee per song, at Mexican restaurants. Many mariachi ensembles begin performing at restaurants in order to practice their skills and to advertise their musical talents. The restaurants serve as stepping stones for jobs performing at family events. Such events include weddings, receptions, birthdays, or parties celebrating accomplishment (e.g., graduation or retirement).

Mariachi instruments have traditionally included a harp, one or two violins, the vihuela, guitars, and a guitarron (Sheehy 1999).The trumpet was introduced to the mariachi orchestra in the 1930s. Today, all instruments except the harp are still visible in a mariachi ensemble. Typical mariachi songs focus on the topics of love, machismo, betrayal, death, politics, and animals. While traditionally mariachi ensembles played songs like *La Bamba* that included a mixture of folk traditions and were associated with different regions of Mexico (Gonzales 1991), mariachi ensembles now play other types of songs such as salsa, cumbia, mambo, and ranchera.

Mariachi Estrellas is managed by Maria, and the members consist of her six children, herself and, at times, two of her grandchildren. The band is run like a family business and each member takes pride in what they mean to the mariachi band. Maria's husband managed a mariachi group for many years. After their separation, she established a band of her own and recruited her children into the group. As they became adults, Maria's children left the group to start their own families. The eldest son, Juan, commented, "I have played the trumpet all my life. I was the first one from my brothers and sister to join my father's mariachi group." Ricardo, Juan's brother, discussed his decision to leave and ultimately return to the group:

> I left the Mariachi Estrellas to spend more time with my family when I got married. However, I always missed being a part of the group. The adrenaline you get when you are preparing for a show and how the public receives you as a mariachi. I longed for that feeling again. (Nowotny et al. 2010: 38)

Sense of place. The Mariachi audience typically participates in the performance. Although, there are some audience members, including Anglos, who participate only as spectators simply by watching the live performance, many audience members actively participate by singing or dancing in close proximity to the mariachi band. It is not uncommon for the vocalist to give the microphone to audience members so that they can sing the song. Jorge, a male from Mexico, commented:

> I like that they put on a show while they are singing. They not only play their instruments but also dance and perform for the audience. They even allow the audience to become part of their show.

When the mariachis play a melancholy song, the dancers join together and sway from side to side at a slow tempo. When the mariachis play upbeat music, dancers will dance around a sombrero or engage in a zapateando, kicking the floor with their shoes. One scene participant, Isabel, commented on the dancing, "This [dancing] allows me to express my love towards the traditions and culture of my heritage" (Nowotny et al. 2010: 38).

As Isabel suggests, the Latinos who enjoy mariachi express a connection or a bond with the music. The music allows them to connect with their Mexican heritage or culture and to reflect back to time spent in Mexico. Rosa, a woman in her fifties who was attending a quinceañera explained:

> I enjoy singing with the mariachi music. She sings very well and her music reminds me of Mexico. It brings back many memories I had when I was living there and when I heard her singing I got caught up in the moment. I had to stand up and start to sing with her because it is a part of my culture and it's a part of me.

Jorge offered a similar observation: "I like listening to mariachi music because it reminds me of my roots. I'm in a country that is not mine. It [the music] helps me forget that I am in United States." Jorge misses his family back home and is says he wants to return soon. But listening to the mariachi music reminds him of Mexico. It brings back memories of the time when he was young, before he left his wife, children, and friends to find work in the United States:

I love this music because it is a part of me . . . I like mariachi music . . .
back home, my friends and I would give gritos when we would hear
mariachi music. In a way, it involves you with the music and with your
past.

Like the conjunto scene, mariachi music accommodates the sense of
places where families congregate, eat, party, and celebrate. Concurrently
and reflexively, conjunto decorates or symbolically outfits the place
where the family is by creating an aura of Mexico, the old country, the
Spanish language and so forth. The Mariachi space is simultaneously
new and old, here and there (Kotarba et al. 2009).

Latino Music: Salsa

Salsa gained popularity in the United States, particularly in New
York, during the 1960s. Salsa combines African and Caribbean rhythms
and almost always involves both singing and dancing. By the 1980s, salsa
was entrenched as a transnational musical genre, popular across the
Americas (Waxer 2002). Latin clubs, radio stations, salsa bands, dancing
schools and dancers are found in numerous countries across the globe,
from Europe to Japan (Bennett and Peterson 2004).

The salsa scene in Houston was established in the 1970s. According to
Julio, a Latin jazz and Salsa DJ, salsa really picked up in Houston in the
late 1970s. There was a single salsa club on the southwest side, and people congregated there to dance and listen to Latin music. People of vary-
ing nationalities—including Caribbeans, Colombians, Dominicans, Puerto Ricans, Cubans, and Venezuelans—all participated in the early scene.
Salsa really exploded in Houston in the 1980s. There were just six Latin
clubs in the city, but the primary salsa club—Cristal—was amazing and
was felt by many to be much like a New York club (Nowotny et al. 2010).

There are two types of salsa venues in Houston: the traditional salsa
club and the Latin restaurant. Salsa clubs are designed around the dance
floor and tend to be upscale with select clientele and a strictly enforced
dress code. These venues are seen as authentic places to dance salsa since
they draw the most acclaimed salsa performers (e.g., Willie Colon, El
Gran Combo de Puerto Rico, and Oscar de Leon). The restaurants that
feature salsa typically serve Mexican cuisine, as would be expected in
Houston. The bands play on small dance floors, allowing for interaction
between the audience and the performers. While individuals do listen to
and dance salsa at restaurants, the primary activity is dining which
makes the atmosphere different from the traditional salsa club.

A unique feature of this scene is the establishment of salsa dance
schools, some of which are located within salsa clubs and some of which
are freestanding dance studios. The first salsa schools opened in Houston
in the early 1990s. These schools are important because they promote the
musical genre to a broader sector of the public and reach beyond just

Latin people. This is largely because dancing is an important feature of salsa music. As Julio Flores, a Latin jazz and salsa DJ, notes: "Dancing is essential in this genre if you want to enjoy the music and have fun in a club." The dance schools significantly contributed to the popularization of salsa among a variety of ethnic groups (Nowotny et al. 2010: 40).

In the 1960s and 1970s, salsa musicians typically played a kind of Son Montuno with lyrics that talked about the "hard life," el Barrio, and urban stories common to people living in big cities. There are legendary characters like Pedro Navaja and Juanito Alimana, both Latin gangsters whose stories were made into songs and popularized by salsa. In the 1980s, however, the salsa market fell. Production of salsa discs was not well received by the public, and salsa lost market share in the Latin music scene. Other Latin genres, like merengue, cumbia and guarachas, became popular instead. In an effort to save the genre and keep their audiences, salsa musicians began to play "Salsa Sensual." Salsa Sensual constituted a new style of playing and singing salsa. The lyrics did not talk about social and urban situations, but instead focused on love and often described sexual encounters between couples and stories about lovers (Nowotny et al. 2010: 41).

The cofounder and director of Orchestra Salerum (a pseudonym) has been performing at Houston venues since 2001. He maintains that the band's main influence comes from salsa, explaining, "While the band plays merengue, bachata, and cumbia, all the musicians are salseros at heart." The issue of authenticity arises when fans and critics alike consider Orchestra Salerum to be a true salsa band with congas, timbales, bongo, full percussion section and four horns that differentiate them from other popular Houston groups. The director elaborated on the authenticity of the group:

> Musicianship is the key, and having the best musicians in Houston wanting to play in your band always helps. . . . We all want to sound authentic and not steer to far away from what the actual recording sounds like. In other words, we are not trying to play the Salerum version of the song. (Nowotny et al. 2010: 42)

Sense of place. The majority of the salsa audience in Houston consists of Latin Americans and Afro-Caribbeans. However, there are an increasing number of Anglos and Asians in the scene, many of whom attend the salsa schools. For example, one elegant club offers salsa lessons prior to the bands performance and coincidentally has the most ethnically diverse audience. Sam, a Japanese national, goes out every Thursday to dance and have fun with his classmates from salsa school. Even though Sam does not understand the lyrics, he learned to feel the music through dance, explaining, "That's the [best] way to dance salsa. The essence of dancing salsa is in you, in what you feel and interpret that sounds in dance steps." For these non-Latino participants, the focus of the salsa music is the emotionality of the dance. As another respondent noted, "All the character of the Latin people is showed when [they] dance Salsa." Carol, an Anglo college student, is also a salsa school student. She loves salsa because the dance is more rhythmical than other musical genres and she admits that people who dance salsa look "elegant and sensual." For both Latino and Anglo audience members, salsa is heavily tied to dance and most participate in the scene because they enjoy dancing and experiencing the music through dance (Nowotny et al. 2010: 42).

The audience at restaurants featuring salsa is more often composed of Latinos, and frequently includes a variety of Latin ethnicities. This audience tends to be older couples or families. Sandro is a middle-age Columbian who frequents one particular restaurant because it is a "nice and quiet place to have fun with [his] family." For Sandro, salsa also reminds him of his home country. He explained that: "everybody in the neighborhood listened to this kind of music. . . . at home, in the public institutions, buses, and even in the streets." Sandro further commented on this idea of being reminded of home, noting that the song "En Barranquilla Me Quedo" reminded him of his city, and the many things he left in Colombia. As he notes: "When I listen to songs about my country, I get goose bumps and innumerable memories come to my mind." The scene allows him to have fun and to experience salsa music through dance. However, it also inspires realistic memories and reminds him of his home country, adding to the scene's authenticity (Kotarba 2009).

It is clear in the Houston salsa scene that salsa has been adopted by people of many different ethnicities. Latin Americans used to feel like they had ownership of salsa (Urquia 2004), but the establishment of salsa schools in Houston has made it easier for non-Latinos to gain entrance to the scene. However, being Latin affords authority when participating in the salsa scene. Urquia (2004) suggests that in the current salsa scenes this authority is challenged by non-Latin people who feel the genre is their own while dancing salsa. The interpretation of salsa by non-Latin people through the introduction of a new dance style has challenged the traditional authentic format defended by the original Latin salseros. Salsa in Houston lost its ethnic association when Anglos, Asians, and Middle Easterners began to challenge the Latin American style of dancing salsa by introducing the New York style as an alternative authority based in dance-class salsa. Nowadays, dance classes shape the nature of the dance and the status associated with different dances. Thus, salsa has become thoroughly cosmopolitan, because it is not limited to only Latino participants and both the music and the dance have changed over time (Kotarba 2009).

Thus, the sense of place for all participants in the salsa scene is the dance floor. It is the "place to be"—a place to have fun with friends, participate in enjoyable activities, and build valuable cultural or social capital (see also Coleman 1988). However, despite the changes to the music and dance and despite the ever-increasing number of non-Latino participants, Latino audience members (like Sandro) continue to feel a deep sense of connection to the music and—like conjunto, Tejano, and mariachi—it reminds them of another place: their home country.

LATINO MUSIC AND THE FAMILY

There are distinct links between traditional Latino music scenes and rock 'n' roll culture. Tejano music, for example, is very much the traditional norteno style music except that Tejano incorporates the rock 'n' roll instrumental components such as amplification and electronic keyboard. Nevertheless, Tejano continues the traditional Latino orientation of family music, or music all generations and members of the family can enjoy. These traditional musical styles function as a thread across generations, nations, and life experiences. In this regard, conjunto and mariachi are very much like other forms of family-oriented ethnic music. We see the same cultural conservatism in polka music, klezmer, and the blues, for example (Kotarba 1998).

The purpose of these forms of music is not to create new cultural worlds, but to preserve the ongoing cultural world. Conjunto and mariachi are family-oriented in two other ways: (1) the music groups themselves are frequently composed of family members, as in the case of Los Monarcas from Houston (who received the 2009 artist of the year award from the South Texas Conjunto Association) and Mariachi Estrella I described above; and (2) the music is utilized at celebrations that typically involve the family like weddings, birthdays, and *quinceañera*. This family orientation is another feature of their authenticity. Interestingly, neither scene is anchored to specific geosocial locations, as Irwin would expect. In other words, individuals do not typically go to a specific place to hear the music, rather the music is brought to a specific place (like a wedding, birthday party, or *quinceañera*) for the purpose of celebration.

Salsa and Latin jazz are similar to one another insofar as their middle-age and older Latino fans increasingly view them as inauthentic due to the invasion of non-Latino participants. Their authenticity is problematic because they are newer musical styles, having emerged in the mid-twentieth century; they have not maintained their original format and musical style, but instead have incorporated new styles and sounds; and they are frequented by non-Latinos who view scene participation as a means of acquiring social capital (see Coleman 1988). These two musical genres do, however, maintain distinctly Irwinian scenes that include both the cultural phenomenon (the artists, audience, music, etc.) and actual ecological locations like clubs, bars, and restaurants.

What seems to unite all four scenes is their conformity to tightly written scripts, as Irwin (1977) predicted about established scenes. One of the most crucial scripts in each of these scenes involves dancing. Participants in each music scene noted the importance of movement and dance to scene participation; in fact, *not* dancing in these scenes would be a violation of the tightly written scripts of the scene and would clearly mark one as an outsider. However, it is important to note that the style of dance varies. In the two highly authentic scenes (mariachi and conjunto), the dancing is informal and spontaneous. However, in the two less authentic scenes (salsa and Latin jazz), the dancing is more formalized. In the case of salsa, for instance, the dance is so formalized that schools have even emerged to teach people the dance steps.

As I mentioned earlier, each of these traditional scenes evokes a unique sense of place. Conjunto and mariachi remind scene participants of a previous time and place, typically of their home country or the land of their ancestors. Salsa also serves this same purpose for many Latino participants. Conjunto and mariachi also serve to create family-oriented places by providing the background and context for important celebrations. Salsa and Latin jazz, on the other hand, are thoroughly cosmopolitan scenes that simply serve as "the place to be" for many individuals from a variety of ethnic backgrounds (Kotarba 2012).

This study of Latino music scenes highlights yet another important feature of the concept of authenticity in the sociological study of popular music (Kotarba 2009). Musicians, composers, critics, and others who create and manage music have a variety of aesthetic criteria to invoke in attributing meaning to music. They all view music in terms of its relative and variable beauty. Authenticity, on the other hand, may be the one distinctively sociological criterion to apply. Authenticity allows us to observe the ways various people position themselves around music in terms of its relative and variable truth. The former approach focuses on pleasure, whereas the latter sociological approach focuses moralistically on the correctness of the performance.

I will argue that the variety of Latino music scenes populated and supported by baby boomer Latinos/as not only offer continuity with the past, but encourage younger members of the community to enjoy the variety of emerging Latino music scenes. These scenes include rock en Espanol and reggaeton, which parents and grandparents in our study generally accepted and supported although rarely participated in themselves. The link across generations and musical styles is the Spanish language that is the source of pride for all members of the typical Latino family.

ADULT EXPERIENCES OF ROCK 'N' ROLL IN POLAND

There is a sharp point of demarcation in adult experiences of rock 'n' roll in Poland.[11] That point in time is 1989, the year that Poland rejected communism and submission to the Soviet Union and chose capitalism and democracy. Before the revolution, general sentiments among adult Poles—and government officials were that (1) rock 'n' roll was a plaything for youth; (2) rock 'n' roll illustrated the worst corruption of Western capitalistic culture; and (3) rock 'n' roll was irrelevant to the progress of Polish culture. Revolutionary fervor changed much of those perceptions. Cultural methods of political resistance, especially rock 'n' roll, among youth in Poland was increasingly seen by adults as one of the most powerful and energetic weapons available for use in seeking independence from Russia. Suddenly, rock 'n' roll, heavy metal music in particular, became a passion for the culturally critical intelligentsia in Poland, emerging as a cultural bridge across generations as well as social classes (Kotarba 2002b).

On the last evening of a visit to Wroclaw in southwestern Poland in 1990, I met a middle-age woman at a university faculty party. She was a professor of existential philosophy at the Wroclaw University. I had heard earlier in the visit that she was a fan of heavy metal music, someone with whom I needed to talk. In preparation for my trip to Poland, I was advised to bring precious rock music cassette tapes with me to distribute as "good guest" gifts. I gave my last good guest gift, a *Faith No More* tape, to her. She loved the tape, and told me that she shared her love for heavy metal and grunge with her seventeen-year-old son. When I told her that this kind of mother-son bond is unusual in the United States, she was dismayed. She noted that elements of Western culture are so intriguing and valuable in Poland that there is no need to invoke unnecessary criteria of taste, just to make a parental point.

Many intellectuals as well as laypersons in Poland view American rock music as a window to American culture and a device for monitoring change in American culture. Poles across ages, genders, and classes are increasingly interested in rap music. Since the revolution, middle-class adolescent girls have become increasingly interested in female artists, less so as sexy role models than as models for women's career accomplishments.

The lyrics imbedded in popular music are especially popular in Poland, since they may possess relevant cultural and political messages of value. In 1993, the hard rock band, Quo Vadis, recorded an extremely popular song called: "Ameryka." This song largely celebrates America by exclaiming its many great accomplishments over a short—by European standards—200-year history. The song states that America is a symbol of freedom for the rest of the admiring world.

The wonder produced by Western popular music is waning a bit in Poland, largely due to the massive changes in media, technology, and the economy that have been taking place since 1989. Cassette tapes are not as relevant as they were before the revolution, when bootleg cassettes were among the very few sources of recorded music in Poland. (Western record companies were leery of attempting to sell legitimate cassette tape recordings for fear they would not be able to recover royalties from the communist government.) The same situation applied to CDs. Since the revolution, access to cassettes and CDs skyrocketed, but the importance of that development is much less today. There is virtually universal access to computers and the Internet in Poland, so that Poles have access to popular music from the west just as it enters Western media: Pandora, rollingstone.com, and so on.

The absence of the traditional time lag in the dissemination of Western pop music to Poland, as well as the expansion of the popular music industry in Poland, seems to result in the return to social class and generational distinction in Polish popular music. An example of changes in adult tastes in popular music, traditional opposition, and criticism of disco polo music among the middle-class has skyrocketed since 1989. Disco polo is the Polish version of simple-to-produce and easy-to-consume pop/party music (Kotarba 2000). Disco polo songs can be mass produced, recorded quickly with only an electronic keyboard for the music tracks. A typical story for disco polo, especially when produced as a video, is celebration of American mass culture—partying on the beach, big and fast cars, and so on. Equivalent styles of music in the United States would include polka music and Tejano music—music for the ethnic working classes. In all my interaction with Poles over the past twenty years or so, I have rarely heard anything but disdain for disco polo. Members of the affluent intelligentsia see disco polo as "low-class peasant music," as one university professor put it.

Now, I like disco polo, much to the chagrin of my university professor friends in Wroclaw, Warsaw, and Krakow. Perhaps my taste is a remnant of my great grandparents' peasant status in southeastern Poland before migrating to the United States in 1917. My point is that conflict over music tastes is a nice indicator of distinctively Polish social class distinctions. The peasants who enjoy disco polo tend to be rural folks, but not "peasants" in any sense of being poor. Peasants in Poland can generate wealth through constantly improving agricultural methods and increasing land values, and can achieve cultural sophistication through an understanding and appreciation for ecologically friendly, natural farming. A major social distinction there is urban vs. rural, which is very much cultural and not necessarily economic.

Sense of Place

Just what and where is the adult rock 'n' roll scene in Poland? A primary scene is the political arena. As Poland moves increasingly into a complex capitalistic economy, military commitments to NATO, and debates over the role of the Catholic Church in Poland's political and cultural life, Poles are learning the proper way to critique a democratic government, and the lesson comes from the good old U.S. of A.: rap music. The case in point is Kazic, who since the fall of communism has been one of Poland's most popular rock 'n' rollers slash rappers. His most significant hit might be a rap video titled "12 Groce." The video is a postmodern masterpiece. Kazic can be seen wearing a cowboy hat and a white T-shirt with the words "Chicago Polish" on the front—is he referring to the famous Polish sausage sandwich popular on the south side of Chicago or someone of Polish ancestry living in Chicago? In any event, the lyrics blast the new Polish regime for, among other things, wasting his tax money on superfluous military adventures while denying assistance for Poland's growing number of heroin addicts. Kazic has become a favorite of baby boomer intelligentsia in Poland who truly appreciate the positive political and economic changes taking place over the past twenty-five years or so, but hip enough to realize one never completely trusts any government to do the right thing at all times (Kotarba 2002b).

The sense of place in adult experiences of rock 'n' roll in Poland is itself truly postmodern: it is enigmatic and very pastiche-like. The eclectic popular music formats and styles made possible by the Internet and media such as Euro-MTV, have opened the door to the revitalization of classic Polish music to be viewed in music video format on TV. Here I am speaking specifically of the renaissance of cabaret as performed, for example, by stars such as Anna Maria Jopek and Edyta Gorniak. The artistic freedom created by the Polish revolution has even created a musical space for Pope John Paul II, one of Poland's favorite sons. He recorded a CD in 1999 titled *Abba Pater*, on which Pope John Paul recites poetry, chants, and sings a bit with a lush Italian orchestral background. This CD was the top selling CD in Poland for over a year. The sense of place in Poland is the complex, ever-changing, romantic, capitalistic yet spiritual world known as Poland.

RAP MUSIC AND POLITICAL RESISTANCE

Rap music has been associated with political activity for many years.[12] There is a long history of rap music in the United States and the Caribbean being used as a medium of political communication. In the 1980s, the American rap group, Public Enemy, performed a very political rap and rap video called *Fight the Power*. This video pioneered the application of the rap idiom rap to urban resistance: "To revolutionize make a change / nothin's strange." Interestingly, Public Enemy called for inclusiveness in the fight against the system: "People, people we are the same."

Groups like Public Enemy have inspired political activists in North Africa and the Middle East during and after the revolutionary Arab Spring of 2011. In the West, political rap music has been very visible on CNN, as are the cell phones carried by protestors in the streets of Cairo,

Alexandria, Tunis, Manama, and Sana'a and used to play the revolutionary rap songs. Advances in the sophistication, affordability, and availability of recording and distribution technology, along with the pervasive availability of cell phones, have led to the timely and efficient production of political rap in the Middle East and North Africa (Kotarba and LaLone 2011). Master Mimz's *BACK DOWN MUBARAK!* was heard up and down the streets of Cairo and Alexandria during the 2011 revolution in Egypt: "It's the rise of people power / Welcome to the 3rd world streets." And the rap concludes with an ominous prediction: "Get outta here—it's our time to shine / Back down Mubarak—Back Down!"

Finally, rap music has become a useful political tool for young Palestinian activists. The group, Dam, have produced a rap video called *Born Here*, in which they decry Israeli oppression in the occupied territories: "Within her (the land known as Old) are those who . . . who destroy / The people who make the mistake of building on their land."

As is the case with many powerful political anthems, a call is made for strong collective, political action to redress grievances: "To take you must demand and / the power is with the collective."

Surprisingly, Dam's rap is popular among young people in both Palestine and Israel. Rap is becoming quite a useful method of communication and empathy across the rigid political lines established by adults and history there—although adults listen to Dam as well. This form of cultural experimentation promises rewards in terms of freedom and democracy. The risks are obvious and typical of any revolutionary activity: political punishment, unfulfilled expectations, and so forth (Kotarba 2012).

Sense of Place

I conceptualize this emerging musical phenomenon as a *hybrid music scene*. Place is not the geophysical location where a scene occurs. As discussed above, place is an outcome of the interaction and music work taking place in a scene. Technology allows a scene to be both local/analog and global/digital simultaneously, as illustrated by the fact that much of the political rap music available in the Middle East is produced by sympathetic friends and colleagues in places like the United States and Great Britain. Technology not only links the participant to a distant event, but also to the immediate event. Technology simultaneously creates and describes an event. The cell phone and the music it can play are here and there (Kotarba 2012).

As mentioned earlier, one remarkable feature of the use of rap in North Africa and the Middle East revolutionary activity is the way it has become the pervasive soundtrack for these revolutions. Although largely produced and disseminated by young people, adults of all ages have taken to rap as a way of portraying their political ideas and feelings. Amir is a sixty-two-year-old electrical engineer from Syria who now lives and works in Austin, Texas. Amir has friends and family in much of the Middle East, and has communicated with many of them regarding the resistance movements. He has recently inquired about the presence of American-inspired rap music there, and his response to me is insightful:

> I don't know rap music. My children know it. They listen to it with their friends from school, I am sure. My brothers in Damascus listen to it. They tell me they look forward to hearing new rap songs about the uprisings. Rap is loud and fast and energetic—the sort of music that tells stories. Our Syrian music cannot do that as well.

TEN

The Recycled Self: The Americana Music Scene

Many of the rock 'n' roll musicians who performed for baby boomers forty and fifty years ago have either stopped performing professionally, have moved into other realms of the popular music industry, or have left music altogether. In this chapter, I will examine baby boomer musicians who continue to occupy the role of artist. Some aging rock 'n' rollers are able to continue performing, largely as oldies or nostalgia acts. They include, for example, groups such as the Rolling Stones, Chicago, Van Halen, Heart, and Joan Jett and the Blackhearts. There are also a number of solo rock performers, such as Paul McCartney, Paul Simon, and Van Morrison, who continue to tour and occasionally record. One message is clear: older bands are, as a group, the most successful live rock music acts performing today. In 2010, the top three acts on the road were Bon Jovi, Roger Waters (formerly of Pink Floyd), and the Dave Matthews Band, grossing a combined $270 million (Knopper 2011).

Americana music is a recent phenomenon in the world of popular music that has done wonders for the careers—and self-identity—of a number of baby boomer rock 'n' roll performers. The genre of Americana music was created in 1995 as a radio format, as a response to the growing dominance of slick, corporate, commercial radio. As Pete Knapp (2011) notes:

> Americana, as defined by the Americana Music Association, is "American roots music based on the traditions of country." While the musical model can be traced back to the Elvis Presley marriage of 'hill-billy music' and R&B that birthed rock 'n' roll, Americana as a radio format developed during the 1990s as a reaction to the highly polished sound that defined the mainstream music of that decade.

The existing styles observable in Americana music include folk, country, rhythm and blues, and rock 'n' roll. On occasion, songs classified as Americana will include ethnic or international influences. The point is that the Americana music scene began as a smart marketing strategy to repackage traditional styles of music performed by aging musicians—often former rock 'n' rollers—without creating, or having to create, any new or innovative musical styles. The Americana Music Association (AMA) produces an annual awards program in Nashville, the Americana Music Festival and Conference. The organization also hosted local music programs and promotions.

The artists identified in this genre traditionally have not fit well either in country or rock—at least in commercial terms. Some of the more significant artists include Lucinda Williams, Rodney Crowell, Willie Nelson, Steve Earle, John Prine, Emmylou Harris, Alison Krauss, Radney Foster, Kelly Willis, Joe Ely, Jimmy LaFave, and Lyle Lovett. A number of Americana artists began their musical careers as rock 'n' rollers, saw their careers run their course, and found—or their agents found—Americana music a great way to revitalize if not recycle their careers and self-identities as musical artists. J.J. Cale, Southern Culture on the Skids, Hans Rotenberry and his band The Shazam are noteworthy. The Americana music scene claims Neil Young as one of theirs, and he is a bit of an exception because his career has remained consistently high over the years. He still fits my argument to the degree he exemplifies the early rock 'n' roller who leaves his rock band affiliations behind over time (e.g., CSN&Y and Crazy Horse) and increasingly forges a solo career and persona that are attractive to the Americana music industry. Many of the older members of this genre were the core of the cosmic cowboy movement in the 1970s and the alt country movement in the 1980s. The following is a press release for a recent club concert by Webb Wilder in Nashville sponsored by the AMA:

> Recently inducted into the Mississippi Musicians Hall of Fame, Webb Wilder has always been an evangelist for real rock 'n' roll. And as a singer, guitarist, bandleader, filmmaker, and humorist, he may be roots-rock's only true Renaissance man. His music is a potent blend of bedrock roadhouse rockers, rootsy blues, lonesome ballads, and crunchy British Invasion grit, all informed by Wilder's distinctly irreverent attitude and wit. The Associated Press described his stage performance as "a glorious amalgamation of grunge chords, killer grooves, Screamin' Jay Hawkins theatrics, a healthy sense of humor, and great pop melodies."

Webb Wilder began his career as a strong rock 'n' roller, fronting a Nashville band known as the Beatnecks. When the Nashville music began shifting to a commercial country music format, Webb shifted his career to a range of activities, including films and film soundtrack work. As is the case with many of the Americana artists, the early personal strategy to engage in a number of entertainment-related tasks to make the semblance of a living became a useful marketing tool to portray the artist as "eclectic."

CASE STUDY: RAY WYLIE HUBBARD

Ray Wylie Hubbard is a grizzly, sixty-five-year-old singer-songwriter who looks like the penultimate old hippie.[13] Ray was born in Oklahoma, and grew up in Dallas, Texas. Hubbard graduated from high school in 1965 and enrolled in college, at the University of North Texas, as an English major. He spent the summers in Red River, New Mexico playing the guitar-based folk music common to the emerging counterculture.

During his time in New Mexico, Hubbard wrote "Up Against the Wall, Redneck Mother," that quickly became an anthem for both the hippie counterculture and the working-class, honky-tonk scene. During subsequent live performances, Ray reconstructs the story behind this song. Briefly, Ray describes how he offered to go to a working-class, "red neck" bar to purchase a case of beer for his friends. The rednecks hassled him a bit because of his long hair and tie-dye shirt—as well as his wise-guy attitude. Jerry Jeff Walker recorded his friend's song in 1973 and it became a national hit. Hubbard recorded several records, but did not attract a broader audience to make for a successful career. Like many of the Americana artists, his mix of country, folk, and blues elements fell between the music marketing cracks, and did not find a sizable audience. After leaving the scene and taking care of some lifestyle issues, Ray returned to recording with *Lost Train of Thought* in 1992 and *Loco Gringo's Lament* in 1994.

Ray Wylie Hubbard's mastery of lyrics-as-poetry and his "cosmic cowboy" mystique have made him an elder statesman of the Texas music scene. His two most recent albums, *Snake Farm* (2006) and *A. Enlightenment B. Endarkenment (Hint There Is No C)* (2010) have been both critical and commercial successes. Ray performed at the 2010 Americana Music Awards, where his most recent album was nominated for album of the year and he was nominated for artist of the year.

How can we explain Ray Wylie Hubbard's recent success? He has, for sure, matured as a person and as an artist. He has evolved into an elegant songwriter and guitar player. *I argue that, like other older rock 'n' roll performers, Ray Wylie Hubbard has garnered success because his total experience of becoming-of-self resembles and resonates well with that of his also aging audience. Changes in the media and entertainment industry have facilitated that conversation by providing meanings to artists and performers that help make sense of self and other.* In order to illustrate this argument, I will briefly describe Ray Wylie Hubbard's live radio program.

"Roots and Branches"

For the past nine years, Ray Wylie Hubbard has hosted a local radio show on Tuesday evenings. The program is broadcast live from 7 p.m. to 9 p.m., from a bar called Tavern in the Greune (pronounced "green") in Greune, Texas, near San Antonio. The bar is standard Central Texas fare: there are Lone Star and Cuervo Gold neon signs all around the otherwise dark room. Rough-sawn wood is present all around the space. The area in back, where the program is hosted, has a small stage and several rows of tables where fans can drink beer while enjoying the program. With his producer, Mattson Rainer, Ray chats with guest artists from the world of Americana Music. The guests usually perform by singing a song occasionally accompanied by Ray on guitar. Typical topics of conversation include the exciting state of Americana music, the sad state of commercial, playlist-driven AM and FM radio, biographical stories, and so forth. We hear stories about the great difficulties artists have breaking into the music business, lifestyle excesses on the road, famous musicians the guests have brushed against over time and, interestingly enough, the wonder of discovering one is more popular in Europe than in one's home state of Arkansas or Kentucky. How to survive the life and the business of music is the most common overriding theme of the program—that is, the miracle of surviving those experiences.

Ray's Fans

Approximately forty fans jam the small room to partake in the program. They must call-in earlier in the week to be placed on the guest list. The audience is largely composed of male-female couples, middle-age and older. There are no instructions to the audience from the producer; the fans seem to know when to clap and when to laugh.

The audience for Ray's radio broadcasts listens to him on the radio religiously. Betty and Mike proudly claim to be long-time fans of southern rock music (e.g., Lynyrd Skynyrd and the Allman Brothers). Betty is a retired school teacher and Mike works for Comal County. Betty spoke for both of them in describing the excitement of actually being at the broadcast:

> This may sound strange, but being here at the Tavern reminds me a lot of the time my mother took us to see Bozo the Clown live at WGN in Chicago. There is nothing like actually being there. . . . It's not the same on the radio or on the TV.

Irene and Curtis drove sixty miles from Austin to take part in the broadcast. Irene works for the State of Texas and Curtis is an insurance agent. For them, the spontaneity of program is refreshing, much like live concerts used to be "in the day." As Curtis indicates:

> I remember when, heck, bands would be late on stage, come on drunk, and forget what they were playing. It was fun; you never knew for sure what you were going to get. Ray's not crazy like that—you know he stopped drinking—but when you see the program you see that there are no fancy scripts or commercials. They go 'til they want to stop and take a break when they feel like it. It's the real deal. . . . Let me tell you one more thing. You don't see Ray and his folks all dressed up fancy like on TV or something.

The scene at the Tavern in the Greune is very much like the blues scene discussed earlier. The audience grew up enjoying live music and drinking beer. As they grew up however, they have come to enjoy their music in comfortable surroundings and circumstances. The Americana middle and lower middle-class audience live and work in or near the big city but are oriented toward country/rural/small town culture. Ray speaks to them as adults, quietly with a bit of self-effacement and survivor's humor ("can't drink like a fish anymore"). This contrasts with the way rock 'n' roll artists addressed them many years ago, with a loud, juvenile swagger tempting them to join in big time, chance-taking partying.

I argue that the popularity of these live radio broadcasts is not primarily the result of an audience that desires to return to some earlier, more pristine time when the broadcast allowed audiences in distant places to enjoy country music performed in settings like the "Grand ol' Opry" in Nashville. Rather, Ray's audience is for the most part returning to the days of their youth when they enjoyed rock 'n' roll music live, even on the radio. They seek the intimacy of sharing in a music performance, not just listening to a recording of one. Other examples of this phenomenon include the dramatic live broadcasts of charity-based festivals, such as Live Aid and Farm Aid several years ago that were immensely popular among baby boomers.

Americana is popular for all the good marketing reasons listed above. I want to propose a phenomenological reason for its success, based largely upon my conversations with baby boomer music fans in Central Texas and the Hill Country, where we live. There is a certain magic and vitality to simply giving something a new name. Many music fans tell me that they have grown weary of the same old names for their preferred styles of music. "Country music" is too commercial and formulaic. "Folk music" is a bit too formal and archaic—these fans do not need any more reminders of the fact they are getting old! "Rock-a-Billy" and "blue grass" are too limiting—and much too southern and not enough western/ Texan. The term "Americana" denotes musical experiences that are contemporary but not pop; meaningful but in a way relevant to aging folks; and accessible to folks who do not like their music over-amplified and or directed to some other—younger—audience.

ELEVEN

The Old Self: Artists and Audiences

In discussing the important place rock 'n' roll has in the everyday lives of baby boomers, I have in fact taken the reader on a voyage across time. We have seen the young rock 'n' roller becoming an old person. Baby boomers are entering the third cycle of their voyage. In the first cycle, children use rock 'n' roll to discover themselves, the world and people in that world. Rock 'n' roll teaches the child that life can be fast, exciting, pleasurable and meaningful. In the second cycle, the adult uses rock 'n' roll to get a second wind on life. Rock 'n' roll provides a window to new worlds when the old ones are getting a bit stale or, perhaps, a bit irrelevant. In the third cycle, rock 'n' roll helps the baby boomer keep all those good feelings and thoughts alive inside "me," as the outside "me" becomes increasingly less hospitable to noise, speed, standing for long periods of time, and imbibing pharmaceuticals not prescribed specifically to control bad cholesterol and high blood pressure.

The continuing chronicling of aging baby boomer rock 'n' roll fans will be a fascinating project. In my research and in my life, I can get a glimpse of emerging patterns. As is commonly the case, the baby boomer seeks and even achieves peace—not only with him or herself and the world, but with rock 'n' roll itself. The value of adhering to strict definitions and styles of rock 'n' roll quickly diminishes as the old timer concludes: it's all good and it's still all rock 'n' roll.

FRIENDS

As one gets old, one really comes to appreciate friends. In middle age, the self-identity of *friend* becomes difficult to maintain. This is especially the case among men, whose hectic and fragmented everyday work/lifestyle does not always leave space for the kinds of friendships typical of childhood and adolescence. Sure, middle-age and middle-class men have business associates, bosses, subordinates, golf partners, and neighbors. But friendships do not always get the time and personal investment needed to thrive.

Gift-giving is a traditional method for nurturing friendships, but what kind of gift can one male friend give another? As mentioned above, one begins to learn the fine art of gift-giving in middle age, but comes to refine it in old age. Enter rock 'n' roll. Many aging men, who spend much time in front of a computer, will burn CDs to give to friends at school, in the neighborhood, and so forth. A gift like this marks a person to self and other as (1) someone who is thoughtful; yet (2) someone who is not caught up in the trivial materialism of gift-giving; and (3) someone who knows his music. In contrast, an inauthentic self is perhaps marked by a gift designed, manufactured, marketed, and thoughtlessly purchased solely as a gift (e.g., a fake Elvis Presley poster purchased at the mall).

As one gets even older, the value of authenticity becomes even more relevant as a feature of the aesthetic and affective bonding occurring through sharing a burnt CD. As I mentioned earlier in this book, I bought a CD of the Van Morrison performance at the Austin City Limits festival in September 2006 and shared it with my next-door neighbor—we're boys! When I moved to San Marcos to take the job as director of the Center for Social Research in 2010, I was greeted and make to feel at home by a CD burnt by a new colleague, Patti Giuffre. Patti is a really big Americana fan, as I am. The CD she gave me as a welcome gift sits in my glove compartment and is played regularly. The James McMurtry song, "Lights of Cheyenne," reminds me of the great feeling I had starting a new job with new people.

Computers, smart phones, iPads ,and other devices are taking over as the primary media for maintaining friendships. Instead of burning and mailing CDs, current technology allows the baby boomer to send music site addresses and the music itself to others. As baby boomers become more sedentary, the volumes of music available on cable and broadcast television will continue to expand exponentially.

GRANDPARENT ROCKERS

In an earlier work (Kotarba 2002a) I wrote about the importance popular music holds for parents as a feature of family interaction, parental control, and so forth. As the baby boomers I studied age, however, their sense of self shifts from parent to that of grandparent. Interestingly, these increasingly senior citizens typically maintain their interest in popular music, although not always in the songs with which they grew up. Being a good or at least competent grandparent in our culture involves doting on grandchildren. Popular music serves as a convenient mechanism for nurturing this kind of relationship. Music is a great gift at Christmas or birthdays. Tickets to concerts are a welcomed surprise for the teenagers in the family.

The example in question is the recent Miley Cyrus/Hannah Montana concert tour in 2007–2008. Robert is a sixty-one-year-old petroleum engineer in Houston. He has two children and four grandchildren, one of whom is an eleven year-old girl who lives close by. Like all her friends and many preteenagers around the country, Sally is a Hannah Montana fan. When tickets went on sale for the concert stop in Houston, Sally wanted to go more than anything else in life. Her parents refused to buy her tickets for, as Robert noted, "they couldn't see spending a hundred dollars or so on a kid concert, and waiting in line for hours to boot." Sally made her plea to Grandfather Bob, in terms of her opinion of what a great birthday present would be. Being the softy he is, Robert obliged, went online, and was very fortunate to be able to buy two tickets at retail—still at a cost of over $100 each. Robert, a widower himself, actually took Sally to the concert. He told me that:

> Sally didn't mind. She had her cell phone with her to talk to all her friends who also went to the concert, during the concert. . . . it was like they all went together! She is way too young to go to something crazy like that by herself.

Similarly, Robert is a life-long Rolling Stones, Led Zeppelin, Cream, and Elvis fan. The inauthenticity of Miley Cyrus/Hannah Montana and her music—as forms of rock and roll—do not bother Robert at all: "It's pretty crappy stuff, but you know, these are just little kids. They do not know any better, what do you expect? It's what they like and what they get on TV. If it makes my little girl smile, then it makes me smile." Therefore, music perceived to be inauthentic does not necessarily mean that the self will find it useless or dysfunctional. Accepting another's inauthentic music may allow grandparents—and other adults if you will—to achieve their ideal self of understanding, caring, and willing to sacrifice one's taste for the good of another person (Kotarba 2012).

ARTISTS

A growing number of aging rockers will devote time and energy to worthy causes. Bonnie Raitt is a good example. She has recently performed gratis for such causes as the Musicians United for Safe Energy benefit concert held in August 2011 in Mountain View, California. Veteran rockers Crosby, Stills & Nash, Jackson Browne, and the Doobie Brothers also performed at this event. Another fashionable thing to do is donate an unreleased song track, to be posted on iTune and downloaded to raise money. Bonnie Raitt and Jon Cleary, for example, donated a previously unreleased, live version of "So Damn Good" from Jazzfest 2009 to benefit the organization, Earthjustice.

Aging baby boomer rock 'n' roll artists seem to tour constantly. Jimmy Buffett, John Mellencamp, Neil Young, Tom Petty, and, of course, Bob Dylan and Paul McCartney come to mind. The crowds for these concerts are generally very large. Veteran rock 'n' rollers can sell out large venues easier than younger performers, who are more dependent on multiple-performer festivals for work (Doyle 2012).

Other aging rockers give up the drudgery of touring for the pleasures of simply being celebrities. The best—and most profitable—way of doing that is to write a book. Most highly visible rock stars have books written about them during the prime of their careers. I am referring now to artists who author their own books about themselves. Perhaps the most publicized of recent rock autobiographies is *Life*, by Keith Richards of the Rolling Stones (Richards 2010). Richards describes a life of chemical excesses, adoration for seminal bluesmen, and what it takes to survive. As a reviewer (O'Hagan 2010) observed, "Richards is cavalier about death—his own and others'—seeing it as a kind of occupational hazard best avoided by 'pacing yourself.'"

CONCLUSION

The last live music event I attended before shipping this manuscript to my publisher was a magnificent performance of Tom Stoppard's marvelous play, *Rock 'n' Roll*, at the Alley Theatre in Houston. The play chronicles twenty-two years of Czech history and examines social and political change in Czechoslovakia and England in the years 1968–1990. The characters are great and very believable to the academics in the audience, such as grad student Jan who returns from England to Prague in 1968 to save socialism, but whose real love in life are the Beach Boys and the Czech band, the Plastic People of the Universe; the angry Marxist professor, Max; and his wife, Eleanor, who teachers poetry; and others who fit right in that revolutionary period in Eastern and Central Europe. It is a great story that we have also heard elsewhere in the narratives about Vaclav Havel and the Velvet Revolution inspired by the Velvet Underground, the Who, and other rock bands of that era.

What caught my attention almost as much as the play itself was the audience. There were a number of old timers in the theater who did not appear to be hip Alley Theatre regulars. They had trouble staying awake—even though Sunday matinees were designed for them—and, since we were in the middle of the swine flu epidemic, seemed to be more concerned with a young child coughing profusely in back than the philosophical discussion taking place on stage.

Now, there have been numerous theatrical performances about rock 'n' roll over the past forty years or so—*Hair, Jesus Christ Superstar*, and so on. Rock 'n' roll is different because it does not play up to current aesthetic and political sensibilities. It is a story about events and ideas as they took place in the past. Put differently, it is almost like you had to live through—survive—the 1960s to understand the play. My guess is that we will see more performances like Tom Stoppard's play designed for us old timers.

I have described several contemporary experiences of self to illustrate the ways the rock 'n' roll idiom has remained a major cultural force in the everyday lives of mature fans. There are obviously other experiences. Furthermore, these experiences are not limited to fans. Rock 'n' roll music is also a preeminent aspect of the musician's self who performed rock 'n' roll music many years ago, and who continues to perform. These musicians redirect their careers in directions more comfortable if not more profitable. Kinky Friedman comes to mind. He was a Texas-based band leader in the 1970s (the infamous Texas Jew Boys). He now performs acoustically in small clubs, while managing a very successful line of men's clothing and authoring popular mystery novels. Is the Kinkster the prototype of a new role for we old rock 'n' rollers: the wise old fan?

There are several rock 'n' roll styles, audiences, and artists underrepresented in this book. The centrality of rhythm and blues, in terms of Motown in particular, is huge and obviously worthy of a book in its own right. Smokey Bill Robinson and the Miracles, the Temptations, Michael Jackson—to understand growing up in the 1960s really requires an acknowledgment of their contribution to our culture. The same can be said for pop music, which we rarely differentiated from rock 'n' roll in our record purchases. Percy Faith's "Theme from a Summer Place" was always on the playlist at our Friday evening parties, ready to stoke a slow dance. There are certainly more women rock 'n' rollers to cover, but I prefer to get into all that in my next work on pop music. Gay rock 'n' roll? How about some nostalgia credit for disco, dance in general, Queen, and all that good stuff from the 1970s?

It has been a great trip—and it still is!

Appendix A: A Lifelong Study

This book has been the love of my scholarly life. My first excursion into the sociological study of rock 'n' roll and popular music occurred in 1984, when I received early tenure and promotion at the University of Houston. Until that time, my worked focused almost exclusively on the sociology of health. I took the opportunity tenure provided me to delve into an area of interest no one could deny me. I designed a course in the sociology of rock 'n' roll, and the rest is history.

As a qualitative and ethnographic researcher operating within a symbolic interactionist framework, I realized that my understanding and appreciation for rock 'n' roll phenomena must be achieved first-hand. In terms of my topic lying under the more general rubric of the sociology of culture, Gary Alan Fine's (1979) concept of *idioculture* nicely summarizes my chosen approach: "Culture is best understood in terms of the ways people use culture in the many possible small groups of which they are members."

The data, insights, and illustrations informing this book are derived from individual and team studies conducted over many years. I engaged in a wide range of qualitative methods including traditional interviews with artists, fans, and producers, participant-observation of rock 'n' roll concerts and events, and the analysis of rock 'n' roll materials and documents.

I refer to my style of research on this topic as *ethnographic tourism* (Kotarba 1994b; Kotarba and Vannini 2009). It is ethnographic to the degree that it attempts to describe rock 'n' roll phenomena in terms of the natural situations in which they occur and in terms of the language, feelings and perceptions of the individuals who experience these situations. This research can be viewed metaphorically as tourism because it is an attempt to approach rock 'n' roll phenomena with wonder and discovery. This analytical distancing of researcher from phenomena is important because the author is a member of the population and culture in question and, as a typical rock 'n' roller, could be too easily tempted to claim experience with and expertise in rock 'n' roll. I have tried to treat all respondents and their musical experiences with awe and respect.

When the researcher assumes that the phenomenon in question is everywhere, then he or she should act like a stranger or tourist in a foreign land. No setting should be taken for granted. No meaning for rock 'n' roll activities should be assumed a priori. The goal is to see the phenomenon where it was previously ignored by both researchers and participants. Rock 'n' roll fits this scenario. My primary research strategy involved observation of ordinary, everyday life activities of ordinary people who enjoy, perform or think about rock 'n' roll.

A methodological premise for my personal accounts of rock 'n' roll experiences is informed by several sources. Autobiographical analyses— or "becoming the phenomenon"—have a long and worthy tradition in interpretive sociology (Jorgensen 1989). Richardson (1990) points to the literary and analytical value of the narrative style conducive to autobiographical analysis. Ellis (1991) encourages the writer of personal narrative to celebrate the deepest feelings underlying yet driving higher order interactional and interpretive work. Ulmer (1989) suggests a particularly relevant genre of discourse he calls the "mystory." A mystory is the account of a personal experience consisting of items from memory blended—for contrast—with cultural representations of those items. The goal is a playful story that reflects the silliness and contradictions of life in the postmodern world. I believe—and hope—that the spirit of the mystory permeates this work.

My first publication in popular music studies was a special issue of *Youth and Society* I edited in 1987, "Adolescents and Rock 'n' roll." The special issue included a report from my first formal music study, "Styles of Adolescent Participation in an All-Ages Rock 'n' roll Nightclub." With the assistance of a brilliant undergraduate sociology major, Laura Wells, I not only learned about heavy metal club music, but also the procedures and strategies for gaining access to the special world of adolescent music.

Although studying young people and their music is a great experience, I have always been intrigued by parents and the complex relationships they have with music. As a young father myself, I was beginning to learn the many ways music permeated family life. My undergraduate students helped me understand the myriad ways music impacted their families; I never encountered a family in which music was neither present nor a factor in everyday life.

My graduate students at the University of Houston contributed in many ways to my methodology and my thinking. Several of them wrote theses on topics ranging from Madonna and reggaeton to DIY bands and rave parties. My graduate students also provided the person power and energy for the Latino music scene study. I assembled a team in the summer of 2007, consisting of seven graduate students enrolled in a practicum. I am extremely proud of the two publications we achieved, on which five of the graduate students are coauthors.

I relocated to Texas State University-San Marcos in 2010. In addition to my teaching position as professor of sociology, I established the Center for Social Inquiry. Taking on new administrative responsibilities did not slow down the continuity of my baby boomer study; in fact, moving to Central Texas helped me put closure on this work. The students at Texas

State are very sophisticated in their music tastes and experiences, at least partially because they live and study in the music-intensive communities of Austin and San Marcos, Texas. The faculty at Texas State are very music savvy. This book may be completed, but I have this sneaking suspicion that the study will go on as long as I do.

Appendix B: Jacquelyn Mitchard's List of "16 Songs Everyone Over 50 Must Own"

- "Once Upon a Time" (Frank Sinatra, 1965)
- "Harvest Moon" (Neil Young, 1992)
- "Lately" (Stevie Wonder, 1980)
- "A House Is Not a Home" (Dionne Warwick, 1964)
- "Little Green" (Joni Mitchell, 1971)
- "Gangsta's Paradise" (Coolio, 1995)
- "Landslide" (Stevie Nicks, 1975)
- "Hotel California" (Eagles, 1977)
- "You Shook Me All Night Long" (AC/DC, 1980)
- "C'est La Vie—You Never Can Tell" (Vocals by Emmylou Harris, 1977)
- "He Stopped Loving Her Today" (George Jones, 1980)
- "For What It's Worth—Stop, Hey What's That Sound" (Buffalo Springfield, 1967)
- "Crazy" (Patsy Cline, vocals; Willie Nelson, lyrics; 1962)
- "God Only Knows" (Beach Boys, 1966)
- "Jailhouse Rock" (Elvis Presley, 1957)
- "In My Life" (The Beatles, 1965)

—*AARP Newsletter*, May 15, 2012

Notes

1. These numbers are gross estimates based on material published on the Internet, through 2012, by sources such as the American Heart Association, the Centers for Disease Control and Prevention, American Association of Retired Persons, and various pharmaceutical companies.
2. This is a revision and expansion of the discussion of men's love songs in Kotarba (1997).
3. Dion recently published an autobiography (DiMucci 2011). His story extends from his childhood in the Bronx to his current lecturing activities as a Catholic.
4. This is an update of my discussion of the positive functions of rock 'n' roll for the family (Kotarba 1994b).
5. See Kotarba 2004 for a complete description of the "Our Parents' Music" project. A major performance of this project is a fifteen-minute, video documentary that I presented at the 2003 Couch-Stone Symposium at Arizona State University in Tempe, Arizona. The documentary consists of conversations between parents and their children regarding their views on, experiences with, enjoyment of, and use of popular music.
6. This is an expansion on my presentation on the KLM prerecorded music system (Kotarba 2005).
7. The "Blues-N-Kids" project was also known as the "Blues-N-Schools" project.
8. This discussion of the "Black Men, Black Voices" project is based on Kotarba (2004).
9. This discussion of rock'n'roll and time is an updated version of Kotarba 2002c.
10. See Kotarba et al. 2009 for a full description of the Latino music scenes study's methodology.
11. This discussion of popular music in Poland is based on Kotarba 2000 and 2002b.
12. This discussion is an initial analysis of the role rap music has played in the on-going conflict of the Arab Spring (Kotarba 2012; Kotarba and LaLone 2011).
13. This biographical statement is informed by an entry in Answers.com, which is perhaps the most comprehensive biographical

statement on Ray Wylie Hubbard available, and a Myspace video, Ray Wylie Hubbard Interview Video, originally taped in 2008.

References

Adorno, Theodore. 1975. "Culture Industry Reconsidered." *New German Critique* 6:12–19.

Adorno, Theodore, and Max Horkheimer. 1993. "The Culture Industry: Enlightenment as Mass Deception." In *Dialectic of Enlightenment*, 120–67. New York: Continuum.

Altheide, David L., and Robert P. Snow. 1991. *Media Worlds in the Postjournalism Era.* New York: Aldine.

Baudrillard, Jean. 1979. *Simulations.* New York: Simeotext.

Baur, Bernard. 2011. *John Michael Talbot: A Biography.* http://www.johnmichaeltalbot.com/biography.php (retrieved October 3, 2012).

Becker, Howard. 1982. *Art Worlds.* Berkley: University of California Press.

Becker, Howard, Michal M. McCall, Lori V. Morris, and Paul Meshejian. 1989. "Theatres and Communities: Three Scenes." *Social Problems* 26:93–116.

Benjamin, Walter. 1936. *Music in the Age of Mechanical Reproduction.*

Bennett, Andy, and Richard A. Peterson. 2004. *Music Scenes.* Nashville, TN: Vanderbilt University Press.

Bergson, Henri. 1922. *Duration and Simultaneity.* Indianapolis, IN: Bobbs-Merrill.

Bering, J. 1993. *Theater, Theory, Postmodernism.* Bloomington: Indiana University Press.

Bloom, Allan. 1987. *The Closing of the American Mind.* New York: Simon & Schuster.

Blumer, Herbert. 1954. "What Is Wrong with Social Theory?" *American Sociological Review* 19:146–58.

———. 1969. *Symbolic Interactionism.* Englewood Cliffs, NJ: Prentice-Hall.

Campbell, Michael. 2009. *Popular Music in America.* Boston: Schirmer Cengage.

Carey, James W. 1989. *Communication as Culture.* Boston: Unwin Hyman.

Castaneda, Carlos. 1971. *A Separate Reality.* New York: Pocket Books.

Cohen, Sara. 1995. "Sounding Out the City: Music and the Sensuous Production of Place." *Transactions of the Institute of British Geographers,* 20, 4:434–46.

Coleman, James S. 1961. *The Adolescent Society.* Glencoe, IL: Free Press.

———. 1988. "Social Capital in the Creation of Human Capital." *American Journal of Sociology Supplement* 94, S95–S120.

Conquergood, Douglas. 1985. "Performing as a Moral Act: Ethical Dimensions of the Ethnography of Performance." *Literature in Performance* 5:1–13.

Couch, Carl. 1985. *Constructing Civilizations.* Greenwich, CT: JAI Press.

Davis, Fred. 1979. *Yearning for Yesterday.* New York: Free Press.

DeNora, Tia. 2000. *Music in Everyday Life.* New York: Cambridge University Press.

Denzin, Norman K. 1987. *The Alcoholic Self.* Beverly Hills, CA: Sage.

———. 1989. *Interpretive Interactionism.* Newbury Park, CA: Sage.

———. 1992. *Symbolic Interactionism and Cultural Studies.* Cambridge: Blackwell.

———. 1997. *Interpretive Ethnography.* Thousand Oaks, CA: Sage.

DiMucci, Dion. 2011. *Dion: The Wanderer Talks the Truth.* Cincinnati, OH: Servant Books.

Douglas, Jack D. 1984. "The Emergence, Security, and Growth of the Sense of Self." In *The Existential Self and Society*, ed. Joseph A. Kotarba and Andrea Fontana, 69–99. Chicago: University of Chicago Press.

Doyle, Patrick. 2012. "Phish, Chilis Invade Bonnaroo." *Rolling Stone,* 1160/1161:17–19.

Ellis, Carolyn. 1991. "Emotional Sociology." *Symbolic Interaction* 14:23–50.

Epstein, John. 1997. *MACHINE.* Seventeen-minute video ethnography.

Erickson, Erik H. 1993. *Childhood and Society.* New York: Norton.

Fabian, J. 1990. *Power and Performance: Ethnographic Explorations through Proverbial Wisdom and Theater in Shaba, Zaire*. Madison: University of Wisconsin Press.

Flaherty, Michael. 1999. *A Watched Pot*. New York: New York University Press.

Fontana, Andrea. 1976. *The Last Frontier*. Beverly Hills, CA: Sage.

———. 1977. "The Existential Thought of Jean-Paul Sartre and Maurice Merleau-Ponty." In *Existential Sociology*, ed. Jack D. Douglas, 101–29. New York: Cambridge University Press.

———. 1980. "Toward a Complex Universe: Existential Sociology." In *Introduction to the Sociologies of Everyday Life*, ed. Jack Douglas, 155–81. Boston: Allyn & Bacon.

Freeman, C. Robert. 1980. "Phenomenological Sociology and Ethnomethodology." In *Introduction to the Sociologies of Everyday Life*, ed. Jack D. Douglas, et al., 113–54. Boston: Allyn & Bacon.

Freeman, Charles, and Andrea Fontana. 1977. "The Existential Thought of Jean-Paul Sartre and Maurice Merleau-Ponty." In *Existential Sociology*, ed. Jack D. Douglas, 101–29. New York: Cambridge University Press.

Friedlander, P. 1996. *Rock 'n' Roll*. Boulder, CO: Westview.

Frith, Simon. 1981. *Sound Effects*. New York: Pantheon.

Gans, Herbert. 1974. *Popular Culture and High Culture*. New York: Basic Books.

Garafolo, Rene. 2008. *Rockin' Out*. 4th ed. Upper Saddle River, NJ: Pearson.

Garfinkel, Harold. 1967. *Studies in Ethnomethodology*. Englewood Cliffs, NJ: Prentice Hall.

Gitlin, Todd. 1987. *The Sixties: Years of Hope, Days of Rage*. New York: Bantam Books.

Goffman, Erving. 1959. *The Presentation of Self in Everyday Life*. New York: Doubleday.

Gonzales, Sylvia. 1991. *History of the Mariachi, Excerpts from Mexico, the Meeting of Two Cultures*. New York: Higgins and Associates.

Grazian, David. 2003. *Blue Chicago*. Chicago: University of Chicago Press.

Greunewald, David A. 2003. "Foundations of Place: A Multidisciplinary Framework for Place-Conscious Education." *American Educational Research Journal*, 40, 3:619–54.

Grossberg, Lawrence. 1992a. "Rock 'n' Roll in Search of an Audience." In *Popular Music and Communication*, ed. James Lull, 152–75. Newbury Park, CA: Sage.

———. 1992b. *We Gotta Get Out of This Place*. New York: Routledge.

Guerra, Carlos. 2001. "The Unofficial Primer on Conjunto." In *Puro Conjunto: An Album in Words and Pictures*, ed. J. Tejada and Alverado Valdez, 3–9. Austin: The University of Texas Press.

Hall, Stuart. 1980. "Cultural Studies: Two Paradigms." *Media, Culture, and Society* 2:57–72.

Haralambos, Michael, and Martin Holborn. 2008. *Sociology: Themes and Perspectives*. London: Collins.

Hebdige, Dick. 1979. *Subculture: The Meaning of Style*. New York: Methuen.

Hill, Trent. 1992. "The Enemy Within: Censorship in Rock Music in the 1950s." In *Present Tense: Rock & Roll and Culture*, ed. Anthony de Curtis, 39–71. Durham, NC: Duke University Press.

Irwin, John. 1977. *Scenes*. Beverly Hills, CA: Sage.

Jameson, Frederic. 1983. "Postmodernism and Consumer Society." In *The Anti-aesthetic: Essays on Postmodern Culture*, ed. Hal Foster, 111–25. Port Townsend, WA: Bay Press.

———. 1991. *Postmodernism, or the Cultural Logic of Late Capitalism*. Durham NC: Duke University Press.

Jaquez, Candida F. 2002. "Meeting la Cantante through Verse, Song, and Performance." In *Chicana Traditions: Continuity and Change*, ed. Norma E. and Cantu and Olga Najera-Ramirez, 167–82. Chicago: University of Illinois Press.

Johnson, John M. 1975. *Doing Field Research*. New York: Free Press.

Jorgensen, Danny L. 1989. *Participant Observation: A Methodology for Human Studies*. Newbury Park, CA: Sage.

Kaplan, Elaine A. 1987. *Rocking around the Clock*. New York: Routledge.

Knapp, Pete. 2011. "What Is Americana Music?" Shuteye Records and Agency. www.shuteyerecords.com/what_is_americana_music.htm (retrieved October 24, 2012).

Knopper, Steve. 2011. "Where Did the Rock Hits Go?" *Rolling Stone* 1125:15.

Kotarba, Joseph A. 1984. "The Existential Self and Society: An Overview." In *The Existential Self and Society*, ed. Joseph A. Kotarba and Andrea Fontana. Chicago: University of Chicago Press.

———. 1987. "Adolescents and Rock 'n' Roll." *Youth and Society* 18:323–25.

———. 1991. "Postmodernism, Ethnography and Culture." *Studies in Symbolic Interaction* 12:45–52.

———. 1992. "Conceptualizing Rock Music as a Feature of Children's Culture." Paper presented at the annual meeting of the Society for the Study of Symbolic Interaction, Pittsburgh, PA, August.

———. 1994a. "The Positive Functions of Rock 'n' Roll Music." In *Troubling Children*, ed. Joel Best, 155–70. New York: Aldine.

———. 1994b. "The Postmodernization of Rock Music: The Case of Metallica." In *Adolescents and Their Music*, ed. Jonathan Epstein, 141–63. New York: Garland.

———. 1994c. "The Rave Scene in Houston, Texas: An Ethnographic Analysis." Paper presented at the annual meeting of the American Sociological Association, Miami, FL, August.

———. 1997. "Four Songs about Women." *Cultural Studies* 2:265–77.

———. 1998. "Black Men, Black Voices: The Culture Producer as Performance Ethnographer." *Qualitative Inquiry* 4, no. 3: 389–404.

———. 2000. "Polish Music: From Chopin to Disco Polo." *iPolonia* 14 (June): 5.

———. 2002a. "Baby Boomer Rock 'n' Roll Fans and the Becoming of Self." In *Postmodern Existential Sociology*, ed. Joseph A. Kotarba and John M. Johnson. Walnut Creek, CA: AltaMira Press.

———. 2002b. "Popular Music and Teenagers in Post-communist Poland." *Studies in Symbolic Interaction* 25:231–44.

———. 2002c. "Rock 'n' Roll Music as a Timepiece." *Symbolic Interaction* 25:397–404.

———. 2003. "Our Parents' Music." Presented at the annual meeting of the American Sociological Association, Atlanta, Georgia (August).

———. 2004. "Our Parents' Music." Multimedia performance presented at the annual meetings of the American Sociological Association, Atlanta, GA, August.

———. 2005. "KLM Flight 0661: Annotating the Existential Self." Paper presented at the annual meetings of the Society for the Study of Symbolic Interaction, Philadelphia, PA, August.

———. 2007. "Music as a Feature of the Online Discussion of Illegal Drugs." In *Real Drugs in a Virtual World*, ed. Edward Murguia, 161–79. Boston: Lexington Press.

———. 2008. "Authenticity and Popular Music." Paper presented at the annual meeting of the International Qualitative Research Association, Urbana, IL, May.

———. 2009. "Pop Music as a Resource for Assembling an Authentic Self: A Phenomenological-Existential Perspective." In *Authenticity in Culture, Self, and Society*, ed. Phillip Vannini and J. Patrick Williams, 153–68. Burlington, VT: Ashgate.

———. 2010. "Coda: Sticking to the Wall." *Cultural Studies—Critical Methodologies* 10:29–50.

———. 2011. "Adult Socialization." In *The Concise Encyclopedia of Sociology*, 589. Boston: Blackwell.

———. 2012. " Taking Chances in Everyday Life: Studying Culture across Continents." In *The Present and Future of Symbolic Interactionism*, ed. Andrea Salvini, Joseph A. Kotarba, and Bryce Merrill, 75–89. Milan, Italy: Franco Angeli.

Kotarba, Joseph A., and Pamela Bentley. 1988. "Workplace Wellness and the Becoming of Self." *Social Science and Medicine* 26:551–58.

Kotarba, Joseph A., Jennifer L. Fackler, and Kathryn M. Nowotny. 2009. "An Ethnography of Emerging Latino Music Scenes." *Symbolic Interaction*, 32, 4:310–33.

Kotarba, Joseph A., and Nicolas J. LaLone. 2011. "Conceptualizing Rap Music in North African and Middle Eastern Revolutions." Paper presented at the annual meeting of the Society for the Study of Symbolic Interaction, Las Vegas, NV, August.

Kotarba, Joseph A., and Phillip Vannini. 2009. *Understanding Society through Popular Music*. New York: Routledge.

Kotarba, Joseph A., and Laura Wells. 1987. "Styles of Adolescent Participation in an All-Ages, Rock 'n' Roll Nightclub: An Ethnographic Analysis." *Youth & Society* 18, no. 4: 398–417.

Kroker, Arthur. 1993. *Spasm*. New York: St. Martin's Press.

Le Blanc, Al "Kool B." 1998. *Deeper Than Blue Ink*. Houston, TX: Wilson.

Lewis, George H. 1983, January. "The Meaning's In the Music: Popular Music as Symbolic Communication." *Theory, Culture and Society*, 1, 3.

Light, Alan. 1992. "About a Salary or Reality: Rap's Recurrent Conflict." In *Present Tense: Rock 'n' Roll and Culture*, ed. Anthony DeCurtis, 219–34. Durham, NC: Duke University Press.

Lomax, Alan. 1993. *The Land Where the Blues Began*. New York: Pantheon.

Lyotard, Jean-Francois. 1984. *The Postmodern Condition*. Minneapolis: University of Minnesota Press

Marcus, George, and Michael J. Fisher. 1986. *Anthropology as Cultural Critique*. Chicago: University of Chicago Press.

Martin, Linda, and Kerry Segrave. 1988. *Anti-rock: The Opposition to Rock 'n' Roll*. Hamden, CT: Archon Books.

McRobbie, Angela. 1978. "Working Class Girls and the Culture of Femininity." In *Women Take Issue*, 96–108. London: Hutchinson.

Mead, George H. 1934. *Mind, Self, and Society*. Chicago: University of Chicago Press.

———. 1938. *The Philosophy of the Act*. Chicago: University of Chicago Press.

Mehan, Hugh, and Houston Wood. 1975. *The Realty of Ethnomethodology*. New York: Wiley.

Merleau-Ponty, Maurice. 1962. *Phenomenology of Perception*. London: Routledge & Kegan Paul.

Moore, Kimberley S. 2012. "Music, Wellness, and You: A Q&A with Kat Fulton ." *Psychology Today*, January 27.

Nowotny, Kathryn M., Jennifer L. Fackler, Gianncarlo Muschi, Carol Vargas, Lindsey Wilson, and Joseph A. Kotarba. 2010. "Established Latino Music Scenes: Sense of Place and the Challenge of Authenticity." *Studies in Symbolic Interaction* 35:29–50.

O'Hagan, Sean. 2010. "Life by Keith Richards." *The Observer*, October 31.

Parsons, Talcott. 1951. *The Social System*. New York: Routledge & Kegan Paul.

Pena, Manuel. 1985. *The Texas-Mexican Conjunto: History of Working-Class Music*. Austin: The University of Texas Press.

Peterson, Richard. 1997. *Creating Country Music: Fabricating Authenticity*. Chicago: University of Chicago Press.

Putnam, R. 2000. *Bowling Alone: The Collapse and Revival of American Community*. New York: Simon & Schuster.

Reese, William A., and Michael A. Katovich. 1989. "Untimely Acts: Extending the Interactionist Conception of Deviance." *Sociological Quarterly* 30, no. 2: 159–84.

Richards, Keith. 2010. *Life*. New York: Little, Brown.

Richardson, Laurel. 1990. "Narrative and Sociology." *Journal of Contemporary Ethnography* 19:126–35.

———. 1994. "Nine Poems: Marriage and the Family." *Journal of Contemporary Ethnography* 23:3–14.

Riesman, David. 1950. *The Lonely Crowd*. New Haven, CT: Yale University Press.

Roof, Wade Clark. 2001. *Spiritual Marketplace: Baby Boomers and the Remaking of American Religion*. Princeton, NJ: Princeton University Press .

Ross, Henry, dir. 1984. *Footloose*. Paramount Pictures.

Rothenbuhler, Eric. 1985. "Program Decision Making in Popular Music Radio." *Communication Research* 12:143–49.

Sartre, Jean-Paul. 1945. *The Age of Reason*. Paris: Gallimard.

Scheer, Greg. 2006. *The Art of Worship*. Grand Rapids, MI: Baker Books.

Scheff, Thomas. 2011. *What Does Love Have to Do with It?* New York: Paradigm Press.

Schutz, Alfred. 1964. *Collected Papers II*. The Hague, Netherlands: Nijhoff.

———. 1967. *The Phenomenology of the Social World*. Evanston, IL: Northwestern University Press.

Seay, Davin, and Mary Neely. 1986. *Stairway to Heaven*. New York: Ballantine Books.

Shank, Barry. 1994. *Dissonant Identities: The Rock 'n' Roll Scenes in Austin, Texas*. Boston: Wesleyan University Press.

Sheehy, David. 1999. "Popular Mexican Musical Traditions." In *Music in Latin American Culture*, ed. John M. Schechter, 34–79. New York: Shirmer Books.

Signoret, Simone. 1978. *Nostalgia Isn't What It Used to Be*. New York: Harper & Row.

Simmel, Georg, and Kurt H. Wolff. 1950. *The Sociology of Georg Simmel*. Glencoe, IL: Free Press.

Sisario, Ben. 2011. "AARP Radio." *New York Times*, July 3.

Storr, Anthony. 1992. *Music and the Mind*. New York: Ballantine Books.

Stucky, Nathan. 1993. "Towards an Aesthetics of Natural Performance." *Text and Performance Quarterly*, 13, 2:168–80.

Stuessy, J., and S. Lipscomb. 1999. *Rock 'n' Roll: Its History and Stylistic Development*. 3rd ed. Upper Saddle River, NJ: Prentice Hall.

"Summer Rocks." 2011. *Rolling Stone* 1134–1135.

Talbot, John. 1999. *The Music of Creation: Foundations of a Christian Life*. New York: Tarcher/Putnam.

Tate, Greg, ed. 2003. *Everything but the Burden*. New York: Harlem Moon/Random House.

Turner, Jonathan H. 1991. *The Structure of Sociological Theory*. 5th ed. Belmont, CA: Wadsworth.

Ulmer, Gregory L. 1989. *Teletheory*. New York: Routledge.

Urquia, N. 2004. "'Doin' It Right': Contested Authenticity in London's Salsa Scene." In *Music Scenes: Local, Transnational, and Virtual*, ed. A. Bennett and R. A. Peterson, 96–114. Nashville: Vanderbilt University Press.

Valdez, Alverado, and Jeffrey Halley. 1996. "Career and Identity in Mexican-American Conjunto Musicians." *Current Research on Occupations and Professions*, 8, 223–46.

Vanderwood, P. 1981. *Disorder and Progress: Bandits, Police and Mexican Development*. Lincoln: University of Nebraska Press.

Waskul, Dennis. D. 2009. "The Importance of Insincerity and Inauthenticity for Self and Society: Why Honesty Is Not the Best Policy." In *Authenticity in Culture, Self, and Society*, ed. Phillip Vannini and J. Patrick Williams, 51–64. Burlington, VT: Ashgate.

Waxer, Lise. 2002. *Situating Salsa: Global Markets and Local Meanings in Latin Popular Music*. New York: Routledge.

Weinstein, Deena. 1991. *Heavy Metal: A Cultural Sociology*. New York: Lexington.

Wilson, Stan Le Roy. 1989. *Mass Media/Mass Culture*. New York: Random House.

Wingfield, Nick, and Don Clark. 2006. "What's Next in Gadgets: Electronics Show Highlights New Twists on E-books, MP3 Players, and HDTV." *Wall Street Journal* (January 5): D1–D3.

Wuthnow, Robert. 2003. *All in Sync: How Music and Art are Revitalising American Religion*. Berkeley: University of California Press.

Yalom, Irving D. 1980. *Existential Psychotherapy*. New York: Basic Books.

Zerubavel, Eviatar. 1979. *Patterns of Time in Hospital Life*. Chicago: University of Chicago Press.

Zurcher, Louis, Jr. 1977. *The Mutable Self*. Beverly Hills, CA: Sage.

Index

About the Author

Joseph A. Kotarba, Ph.D., is professor of sociology and director of the Center for Social Inquiry at Texas State University-San Marcos. He received his doctorate from the University of California at San Diego. Dr. Kotarba's scholarly focus is the sociology of everyday life, and he works primarily in the areas of culture, health, and existential social theory. His current projects include a study of the culture of translational scientific research at the University of Texas Medical Branch in Galveston, Texas (funded by the National Institutes on Health); and a study of the delivery of emergency medical care to musicians and their fans. Dr. Kotarba is the author or editor of seven books, and over ninety-five articles and book chapters. He is the 2009 recipient of the Society for the Study of Symbolic Interaction's George Herbert Mead Award for Lifetime Achievement. Dr. Kotarba is also the 2010 recipient of the Society for the Study of Symbolic Interaction's Mentor's Excellence Award. His most recent book is *The Present and Future of Symbolic Interactionism*, coedited with Andrea Salvini and Bryce Merrill (2012).